DÓNAL DONNELLY

PRISONER '1082'

Escape from Crumlin Road, Europe's Alcatraz

D1300438

The Collins Press

FIRST PUBLISHED IN 2010 BY
The Collins Press
West Link Park
Doughcloyne
Wilton
Cork

Reprinted 2010

British Library Cataloguing in Publication Data

Donnelly, Donal.
    Prisoner 1082 : escape from Crumlin Road Prison
    ('Europe's Alcatraz').
    1. Donnelly, Donal. 2. Crumlin Road Prison
    (Belfast, Northern Ireland) 3. Irish Republican
    Army–History.
    4. Escapes–Northern Ireland–History–20th
    century.
    5. Political prisoners–Northern Ireland–Biography.
    6. Fugitives from justice–Biography.
    I. Title
    941.6'0823'092-dc22

ISBN-13: 9781848890312

Typesetting by The Collins Press
Typeset in Bembo
Printed in Great Britain by CPI Cox & Wyman

Cover photos courtesy of the author

CONTENTS

DEDICATION

This book is dedicated first to John Kelly of Belfast and Maghera whose friendship I was privileged to enjoy. He played a major role in this story and I remember his personal courage and tenacity. He committed himself throughout his life to speaking up fearlessly for those marginalised or isolated, and he had a keen sense of justice. He lived a full life and died aged seventy-two in 2007. *Go ndéana Dia trócaire ar a anam uasal.* The book is also dedicated to those brave and often nameless people and their families in Belfast, Dungannon, Donaghmore, Altamuskin and Monaghan who assisted me fifty years ago at great personal risk to themselves to ensure my freedom. I will never forget them.

ACKNOWLEDGEMENTS

First I would like to thank my grandchildren, Aaron and Alanna Donnelly, now eighteen and fourteen respectively, for ensuring that my memory of events of fifty years ago has remained intact. Their insistence on hearing my story over and over again at bedtime, and even participating in its telling, is a beautiful memory. I am also indebted to our latest grandchild, Daniel Joseph Cullen (Danny), born in February 2009, whose company and fantastic smile in the last year of the writing of this book was a constant source of encouragement and joy. Before them our own children, Eoin, David, Úna and Deirdre, had enjoyed the story and even told it frequently to their disbelieving teachers and school friends. They are always very encouraging and supportive. Also a big thank you to my brother Jim, who lives in Cambridge, and who kept a scrapbook of the newspapers of the time and memorabilia such as prison visitors' cards which he presented to me many years ago. The scrapbook was invaluable when writing this book.

Anthony Glavin, writer, author and editor, gave me constructive advice at the outset which was critical to the publication of this book. We first met, appropriately enough, at the Benedict Kiely Literary Weekend, held every year in Omagh. I wish to thank and acknowledge the research work carried out by my second cousin, Sarah Gallagher McKiernan, whom I only got to know in recent times. She provided a steady stream of photographs, family stories and some unique background detail which had eluded me. A neighbour from my schooldays, Jackie McGale, was unstinting in his support. He researched reports of numerous events and also provided photographs. Jackie is an author and poet of note and has published books on various aspects of Omagh life. Thanks also to Maura and Seán Gaynor of Dublin for their photographs. I would like to record the invaluable assistance provided to me by Oliver Kelly (Belfast), who has since passed away, and his brother, Jimmy, and wife, Nora, who helped me complete the story.

For their time and hospitality I thank my old comrades from the Omagh district, Fergus McCabe, Jim Darcy, Jim Devlin, Hugh Darcy, Arthur McCarroll and Frank Cullen. I had the pleasure of meeting Teddy Devlin and Plunkett O'Donnell of Dungannon again and listening to their graphic descriptions. A special thanks to Paddy Joe (P. J.) McClean of Beragh, who was generous with his reminiscences and advice. P. J. is the subject of an excellent short film made by his daughter on his experience of internment in 1956. He and his wife, Annie, were the perfect hosts when I called. I wish also to thank Jim Lane and Brendan O'Neill from Cork both for their oral testimony of our shared experiences and their written record of that and other events around the same time. They have their own story to tell and no doubt it will be told. I wish also to thank Brian Ferris and his family from Glenhordial who are always so supportive. My conversations with very good friends Eddie Mulholland originally from Lurgan, Anthony Cooney, Cork (now Germany), Frank McArdle, Ballymena and Dan Moore, Dublin, originally from Newry, about our common experiences in Crumlin Road Gaol were very instructive to me in writing about that period and I am grateful to them. Listening to Charlie Murphy, Noel Kavanagh and the late Gerry Higginbothem, all from Dublin, talk about their experiences at the hub of events in the 1950s provided me with an additional aspect.

Our good friends Brendán Ó Flannagáin and his wife,

Nancy, were especially helpful with their memories and anecdotes. Although living in Dublin since 1940, both Brendan, who is originally from Omagh, and Nancy from Dungannon have a lively interest in developments north of the border. Monsignor Raymond Murray contributed uniquely to the history of the 'Troubles' with his many publications on the injustices perpetrated by the state and others. He worked courageously on behalf of those unjustly punished and the families of those murdered. His name and that of the late Monsignor Denis Faul are bywords for justice for all. Many of their personal papers are now held in the relatively new Cardinal Ó Fiaich Library in Armagh. I thank Monsignor Murray for his advice. All those mentioned gave generously of their time. I wish to thank Des Crowther of the Irish Institute of Purchasing and Materials Management for photographs.

The Public Record Office of Northern Ireland personnel were most helpful and both the detail of their records and their accessibility was a pleasant surprise. University College Dublin Archives Department was a great source in relation to the Humphreys family, whose papers and diaries are kept there. The National Library of Ireland provided records of newspapers which contribute specifically to a particular chapter. The staff there were most courteous and helpful. Liam Barr, Project Manager with the Northern Ireland Department of Social Development, whose task is the regeneration of Crumlin Road Gaol and district, allowed me into the prison several times to take photographs and confirm my memory. The department's staff also permitted my daughter Úna to film extensively there.

Saol (Life), an Irish-language news magazine supported by Foras na Gaeilge, published an interview with me in a two-part series in 2007 which presaged the content of this book. To its editor, Colm Ó Torna, *go raibh míle maith agat.*

A prison officer who worked in Crumlin Road Gaol in the 1940s, 1950s and 1960s, but who would prefer to remain unnamed, kindly shared his memories with me. Over the period of writing this book a great friendship has developed between us and also our wives, which we treasure.

I want to thank The Collins Press for their forbearance and support when our agreed schedule was unexpectedly upset. My son-in-law, Julian Cullen, made an inestimable contribution to my being able to deliver this book. He gave generously of his many talents over a long period. Finally I want to thank the love of my life, my wife Caitríona, for proofreading, making suggestions and giving good advice. Her contribution was enormous and I am greatly indebted to her for her patience and support.

INTRODUCTION

This book tells the tale of a dramatic incident during the 1956–'62 campaign of resistance to British rule in Ireland. The story told is much more than that. It places the author and the campaign in its proper historical setting. Many young men throughout Ireland were persuaded that only by taking up arms could justice be achieved. The social, political and historical influences that convinced them are set out here. In that context the personal and family history is also included to explain why two young men found themselves on the top of a prison wall on a bitterly cold winter's night at risk of being shot dead by police marksmen stationed in the prison's gun turrets. The story is one of success but also failure. One of the success stories centres on 'the one that got away'. I did not achieve it on my own; courageous people in Belfast, Tyrone and Monaghan contributed to my escape against all the odds. They placed themselves and their families in danger by providing shelter, transport and cover for a fugitive most of them had never met. But why did they take such risks for no benefit to themselves? The reason is explained in this book and, as a result, begs the question: why did the British government ignore all the warning signals?

In the mid-1950s thousands of respectable people in Mid-Ulster voted not once, not twice, but three times for a 'convicted felon' in Crumlin Road Gaol. This should have told the government that there was, to paraphrase the Bard, 'something rotten in the state of Northern Ireland'. The

people were convinced that no one was listening, least of all
the government, who claimed that the six-county state was
'an integral part of the United Kingdom'. The government
served only one section of its own citizens. If it had acted then,
it is quite possible that not only would the campaign of
resistance – known as 'Operation Harvest' –never have taken
place but neither would the thirty years' war between 1968
and 1998. There was also a responsibility on the Unionist
parliament in Stormont to deal promptly and transparently
with the fundamental issues of 'one man, one vote' and other
forms of discrimination. The politicians did not rise to the
challenge and were humiliated throughout the world in later
years by having their parliament prorogued by their own allies,
a Tory government in London, as not being fit to govern. The
lesson is universal – take care of your minorities and do not let
injustices fester.

The book also provides a unique record of the British
penal system in the mid-twentieth century by someone who
experienced it at first hand. I spent my eighteenth, nineteenth,
twentieth and twenty-first birthdays in Crumlin Road Gaol.
I describe in detail the nineteenth-century layout of the prison
and the modus operandi of the Governor and his staff. Two
men were executed in the prison in 1961, a year after my
escape. These were the last executions to take place in
Northern Ireland. The book describes the conditions and the
daily routine, making an important contribution to the penal
history of the last century.

Many of my fellow prisoners were among the leadership
of the Provisional IRA and the Official IRA, none more
prominent than my fellow escapee, John Kelly, the Belfast
republican who featured so often in the events that have
shaped the 'new dispensation' in the Six Counties. The
narrative provides part of the genesis of the rise of the
northern republicans in the years following my incarceration.

Finally, the book follows my move from participation in
physical force solutions to involvement in highlighting

injustices elsewhere in Irish life. My escape was a severe embarrassment to the British but also to a minority among the IRA leadership within the prison, as it was not authorised by them. Consequently, the event has been practically airbrushed out of Northern Ireland history and, amazingly, out of authorised republican history also. Down the years a common question was: 'Whatever happened to the man from Gallows Hill?' This book tells that story. This is my memoir.

A SHORT CHRONOLOGY OF IRISH HISTORY

Included here is a thumbnail sketch of Irish history for readers who may not be familiar with the context. Very early dates are approximate. History is often popularly discussed in simplistic terms but behind apparently straightforward facts lies a mound of complexity. This summary is no exception.

BC   (Before Christ) There is no record that the Romans ever invaded Ireland.

AD 432   St Patrick arrives to convert Ireland to Christianity.

800   Vikings come to colonise Ireland.

1014   Brian Boru defeats the Vikings at the Battle of Clontarf.

1155   English Pope (Adrian IV) issues the Bull *Laudabiliter* granting King Henry II of England permission to reform the Church in Ireland.

1169   Anglo-Norman forces invade the Irish province of Leinster.

1172   The English occupation of Ireland begins with a royal charter establishing overlordship.
          Ireland remained for many years a land of tribal chiefs who governed their own specific areas and only came together to fight a common foe. From this year onwards England was the main enemy and skirmishes, campaigns and wars were fought continuously, with occasional seminal events

which changed the course of Irish history.

1536   Henry VIII's Reformation Laws applied to parts of Ireland, with the suppression of Catholic monasteries. During the reign of Henry VIII the split with Rome created the Protestant and Catholic divide. While England, for the most part, acquiesced with Henry and his new religion, the Irish did not.

1558–1603 The rule of Elizabeth I, daughter of Henry VIII, causes much hardship in Ireland, resulting in several uprisings against English rule.

1586   Large plantations begin and continue in later decades as English people are given the lands of the native Irish. Thousands of English and Scottish settlers usurp the good lands of the native Irish and bring to the country their new religion.

1592   Red Hugh O'Donnell escapes from Dublin Castle and later joins in the Ulster rebellion against the English.

1598   The forces of O'Donnell and O'Neill defeat the English at the Battle of the Yellow Ford.

1601   Defeat for the Ulster chieftains at the Battle of Kinsale when the Spanish Armada, which comes to their aid, is also defeated. The 'Flight of the Earls' takes place in 1607.

1641   Irish Catholics fight back and rebellion spreads.

1646   Owen Roe O'Neill defeats the English in the famous Battle of Benburb.

1649   Owen Roe O'Neill is poisoned and dies. Oliver Cromwell arrives in Ireland and begins his campaign of massacre. While claiming to be a republican in England (he executed King Charles I in 1649), his name will forever be vilified in Ireland.

1650–9   The Act for Settling Ireland sets out draconian punishments for the Irish, including forfeiture of

	their land and banishment to the West Indies and to the province of Connaught, where the land is very poor.
1658	Oliver Cromwell dies.
1690	A war between two English kings, the Catholic James II and the Protestant Dutch William of Orange, culminates in victory for William at the Battle of the Boyne, an event celebrated on 12 July each year by the Orange Order in Northern Ireland.
1697 & '98	Additional Penal Laws forbid Catholic graveyards and banishes Catholic clergy. Penal Laws were aimed at reducing the Irish to the condition of slaves.
1798	Wolfe Tone and his United Irishmen, most of whom are Presbyterian, rebel against English rule with the slogan 'Break the connection with England'. They are defeated and the French navy, which had sailed to support the rebellion, scattered in Donegal Bay.
1800	The great betrayal. The Act of Union between Ireland and England is approved by means of threats and bribery.
1803	Robert Emmet's rebellion is defeated and its leaders hanged.
1829	Catholic Emancipation is enacted and Daniel O'Connell, 'The Liberator', takes his seat in Westminster parliament the following year.
1836	The Royal Irish Constabulary police force is formed. (It was dissolved in 1923.)
1845–50	Famine results from the potato crop failure, while grain is exported. One million people die of hunger and plague and another million emigrate to America. Neglect by the British authorities is blamed for the Famine, which leaves an indelible scar on the Irish psyche.

1867   The Fenian uprising is defeated. Catholics in the North were forever after called 'Fenians' by loyalists using it as a derogatory term.

1879   The Land League is formed seeking the 'Three Fs': Fair Rent, Fixity of Tenure and Free Sale. The country is mobilised, with Michael Davitt and Charles Stewart Parnell as leaders.

1884   The Gaelic Athletic Association (GAA) is formed in Thurles, County Tipperary. The association has grown to become the largest amateur sporting organisation in the world.

1889   The Pioneer Total Abstinence Association is formed by Fr James Cullen. It leads to thousands of Irish people leading sober lives.

1893   The Gaelic League (Conradh na Gaeilge) is founded in an effort to encourage the speaking of Irish. (The Land League, the GAA, the Pioneer Association and the Gaelic League were the harbingers of a more confident Ireland, and all contributed to the eventual 1916 Rising and the War of Independence, 1918–22.)

1916   An uprising with its headquarters in the General Post Office, O'Connell Street, Dublin ends in failure. However, the execution of the leaders galvanises the people in support of a bloody conflict with the British, known as the Black and Tan War or War of Independence (1918–21).

1921   Treaty with England gives independence to twenty-six counties of Ireland while creating a border between them and the six northeastern counties known as Northern Ireland. Stormont government is introduced in the North, described as a Protestant parliament for a Protestant people. (It was dissolved in 1972 by the British government.)

1922–23   Civil War among republicans results in victory for the pro-Treaty forces and the formation of the two competing political parties that between them have ruled the twenty-six counties for most of the past eighty-six years – Fianna Fáil (anti-Treaty) and Fine Gael (pro-Treaty).

1937   New constitution adopted by the Irish people.

1939   Second World War begins, during which the twenty-six counties remain nominally neutral. The IRA begins a bombing campaign in Britain during the war.

1949   The twenty-six counties officially become the Republic of Ireland.

1956–62 Another IRA 'resistance campaign' begins – Operation Harvest.

1968   The Civil Rights campaign begins in Northern Ireland. Its aims are universal suffrage in local government elections, an end to religious discrimination in housing and jobs and the disbanding of the B Special constabulary.

1969–98 Provisional IRA 'armed struggle' against British rule in Ireland.

1998   IRA ceasefire in 1997 is followed by the Belfast Agreement (also known as the Good Friday Agreement) which was validated by the people on both sides of the border – by over 94 per cent in the Republic and over 70 per cent in Northern Ireland. For the first time since 1972 the Stormont government is restored, but under very different conditions.

1

EUROPE'S ALCATRAZ

Crumlin Road Gaol in Belfast was famed as the most impregnable in Europe in the 1950s and 1960s. The recommendations of a special security committee had just been implemented, including new wall lighting outside individual cells on A Wing, new fluorescent lighting within the prison and the closing off of A Wing by raising the wall 6 feet. Gun turrets on each corner of the outer walls, manned twenty-four hours a day, were already a feature. The high-security A Wing housed political prisoners as well as 'ordinary' criminals, many of whom had death sentences for murder reprieved.

Despite all this security, two of us had a plan, and on a cold winter's evening in 1960 we were on top of the outer wall of Crumlin Road Gaol. Conscious of the marksmen who manned the two gun turrets we eased our way along the slippery connecting wall towards the outer wall. We had to stop to draw breath as sleet and wind hampered our progress. Our clothes were totally inadequate for the weather – shirt, trousers, heavy woollen socks and light rubber slippers. We heard armed officers in the inner yard as they good-humouredly jostled one another to keep themselves warm. Because of an unfortunate incident with our long rope, the only plan left was a hastily concocted one fraught with danger. One of us would hold the remains of the rope as an anchor while the other lowered himself down the 25-foot wall. I went first while John Kelly from Belfast held the rope. As the rope received my full weight, it broke. I fell outside the wall on to a concrete base while John fell back inside the prison. I was free, but could not move.

It was St Stephen's Day, 26 December, also known as Boxing Day. Earlier that evening we had all watched a film in the common room, which was also used as a church, chapel and concert hall. After tea we were allowed two hours' recreation in the dining hall. In A Wing dining hall prisoners played table tennis, snooker, cards or just chatted, under the watchful eye of three warders. The mood was relaxed and there was an air of relief as Christmas Day had now passed – Christmas can be a sad time for those in prison, away from family and friends. At 5 p.m. John Kelly from Adela Street in Belfast and myself had separately raised an excuse to go to our cells to fetch a table tennis ball and, for my part, a table tennis bat. Prisoners could only leave one locked area for another under supervision. The warder was very reluctant to let us out at all, especially at the same time, but eventually allowed John out and after a few minutes called to the warder in A Wing that he was sending me out there. This was the vital access we needed. 'One off,' they would call, and the receiving officer would reply 'One on.' Instead of going to my own cell on A3, on the third storey of the wing, I went to John's cell on A2. Prisoners were not allowed to go into other prisoners' cells and the warder was already shouting, 'Donnelly, where are you going?' I answered, moving quickly, that I was collecting a table tennis bat. He followed me up the stairs but got distracted, which left the coast clear to John's cell. The cell was in darkness and John was still attempting to finish the work we began on Christmas Eve – cutting the bars. Standing by was our good friend Séamus McRory from Ballymena whose task was to throw our coats into the yard when we dropped from the second storey. We had cut the bars with hacksaw blades but the biggest obstacle was the steel frame that acted as a weather barrier with inserts of small rectangular panes of glass. It was particularly difficult to cut as the surface was thin and uneven, and cutting it produced a sound akin to a cat in pain. We had determined that four cuts on the bars and window frame would allow sufficient room for us to squeeze out one by one.

The authorities were always delighted when a prisoner washed his cell out. So just before Christmas John and I had put our names down with our individual class officers for such permission. My cell was located directly above John's, and when John began to cut the bars I began cleaning my table in the corridor outside my cell with a borrowed scrubbing brush, making sure my scrubbing drowned out the sound of the cutting below.

On St Stephen's Day we had to finish cutting the window frame to facilitate our exit. This created some noise, which could not be prevented. John pulled the cut section of the bars into the cell and forced the frame back with a large bumper handle. I climbed on top of the bedstead which stood against the wall and on to the slanting window sill. Many aspects of the prison architecture – including the slanted window sills – made escape almost impossible. But we were both young and physically very fit – John was twenty-four and I had just 'celebrated' my twenty-first birthday three months earlier. Now with my head and shoulders outside the bars I could feel the exhilarating tingle of sleet on my face. We had done it.

My satisfaction was short lived, however, as by now the warder was in full pursuit of me, bawling out 'Donnelly, Donnelly, where are you? Back to the dining hall immediately.' We knew we had the element of surprise and the three of us could have easily overpowered him. But it was not in our plan and no thought had been given as to how we could secure him after we quietened him, so I crawled back into the darkened cell. 'Leave it to me,' I said, as we heard the warder approach. I placed my hand on the peep hole in the door to prevent him from seeing the hole in the window silhouetted by the outside lights. At the same time I pulled the door open slightly and had the nerve to say 'Boo!', letting on that I was only hiding on him. But he was not so easily fooled. He demanded to know why I was there and my excuse was that we were having an Irish class; we had placed books on the table to create that impression. He insisted that we either go to the dining hall or choose to be locked in our separate cells. I knew that if we returned to the dining hall the warder there would not let me back up the stairs. Jails are mostly fussy, busy places, but when the warders are attempting to secure their exact numbers they can be very tense. I made a decision, telling the warder that I would prefer to be locked up in my cell. A quick, unnoticed consultation with John agreed a plan that both of us should seek to be unlocked in a few minutes to go to the dining hall. The situation was excruciating, as we would be separated with no chance of communication.

As we sat in our individual cells we could hear the noise in the wing, with bells ringing, and knew there was no guarantee that the warder would respond to our call to be released or agree to do so. After what seemed an eternity (it was about fifteen minutes) I heard John's bell ringing below. Prisoners were discouraged from ringing the bells, since at night time the warder needed to be accompanied by another officer, which upset their timetable. It was used, therefore, only when someone became seriously ill. That St Stephen's Day seems to have been an exception, however, as several other bells sounded apart from ours.

As soon as I heard John's door being opened I assumed that he had been allowed to return to recreation, and so pressed my own bell. My hope was that it would distract the warder, Mr Rampf, and that John could sneak back into his cell while the officer came to see what I wanted. That is how it panned out. The warder came to my cell a bit frustrated. 'First you want to be locked up and now you want to go to recreation. Do you think I have nothing to do but run around after you?' He kept a constant watch on me as I descended the two flights of stairs on my way to the dining hall. When satisfied that the recreation hall warder had me in his sights he stopped looking and continued with another task.

As I came to the end of the stairs which ran down from the centre of the wing, I turned and began running up again saying, 'Oh, I forgot my table tennis bat.' The warder shouted back, 'Donnelly, come back here', but I knew he was en route to another check and would hardly trouble me again for at least three or four minutes. That is all the time we needed. I ran immediately to John's cell. 'Let's go,' I said and climbed onto the slanting window sill again and, with the rope hanging loosely around my neck, secured one end to one of the solid bars. I abseiled down the two storeys to the ground, leaving the rope in place for John and holding the bottom end firm.

We were now in the yard nearest the outer wall, in the driving sleet. The temperature was a shock to us since, for the past four years, we had never been out in the dark during the winter. Séamus McRory was unable to throw out our coats as he was forced to create a diversion when the warder returned to the cell door. Séamus, a first cousin of the writer Frank McCourt, critically informed the warder that both John and I had already gone down to the recreation hall. We were unaware of what was going on in the cell we had just vacated, but quickly realised that we would have to do without our jackets.

Looking around, we saw that some cells had lights on, but there were no lights on in the administration block, our first target, apart from an illumination in the main corridor. There was no activity or movement anywhere in the yard, which meant that we were on our own. We did not wait long because we knew something had happened inside. We began to crawl along the open surface water drain towards the administration block, situated in the centre of the prison. The drain was cut deeply into the ground and the raised garden of grass and flower beds provided us with added protection. This was a crawl of some 200 metres. Wet, cold and bedraggled, we eventually reached the first window of the administration block which housed the Governor's office, the common hall and the reception area which buzzed with activity during the day. Internally the administration block leads to the Circle, from which the four wings of the prison spread out. The building was in darkness except for an illumination in the main corridor.

With our rope made from torn blankets, sheets and electric flex we began the ascent of the three-storey building. First John climbed the bottom window, whose horizontal and vertical bars acted like a ladder. With John positioned on the top horizontal bar I climbed on to his shoulders like an acrobat to reach beyond the jutting-out ledge and grab the bottom bar of the second window before hauling myself precariously on to the second window ledge. We had identified this manoeuvre as critical to our plan. I then lowered my rope to allow John to join me at the second window. This window was the platform for our escape. In the authorities' eagerness to make Crumlin Road Gaol the most impregnable in western Europe they had increased the height of the outer wall by a number of feet. They had also raised the inner semicircular wall which closed off A Wing from access to the front gate inner area. This new inner wall was raised to the same height as the outer wall. This actually worked to our advantage, as the window right beside the new wall which we were now on was the perfect launching pad for an escape. The armed police in the gun turrets could not see that part of the administration block because of the laundry, tailors' workshop and cobblers' workshop building, while the armed police in the D Wing turret, where the internees were held, could not see it since it was on their blind side.

The plan had gone very well up to now and our only concern was time – we knew that the continuous counting of prisoners which is a feature of all prisons would eventually highlight our absence. We had lost some valuable time because of the attention of the A Wing warder. Now as John caught the lowering rope to raise himself up, the first unplanned incident occurred – a portion of the 70-foot rope fell on to the wrought iron railing over the tunnel linking the prison to the courthouse across the road. The rope fell through the railing and became entangled. John and I pulled vigorously on the rope to free it, but it broke and we were left with the weaker portion in our hands. The original plan was to anchor the rope to the bars of the second-floor window where we were out of sight of the gun turrets and then, bringing the rope with us, move quickly across the linking inner wall to the outer wall and drop safely into the outside world.

One Out, One In

Every Christmas Day we were locked up for twenty hours out of the twenty-four. As the authorities said, the warders needed the time off to be with their families! On the evening of that Christmas Day I had begun to make the rope in my cell. It was a precarious activity as the warders checked the cells every half hour by looking in the peep hole and moving on quietly to the next cell. When the lights were out they shone their flashlamps through the second aperture in the door. Some warders wore slippers at night, possibly for comfort, which made it difficult to hear them. The new security lighting outside my window offered sufficient illumination for the task at hand. From midnight I sat on the floor intertwining the flex and blankets. But the constant checking of our cells and other noises prevented me from completing the job. In anticipation of each check I had to jump into bed and pretend to be asleep, and allow some time in case the warder returned, which sometimes he did.

The security pattern in the prison was impressive. There were daily unannounced searches of people and cells and contact between warders and prisoners was on a strictly professional basis; indeed many of the political prisoners avoided any unnecessary contact. The authorities had also installed fluorescent lighting within the prison and spotlights on the walls outside the A Wing cells. It was when that work was taking place that I acquired hundreds of feet of electric flex.

John and I knew before we set out that the tail end of the rope was weak, but this did not present a problem as we reckoned we could jump the last 10 feet. The rope had already proven robust as we had used it to drop from John's cell to the yard. After the rope broke, however, things got even worse when the light went on in the stairway to the common room (the chapel). John was still on the first window and I was on the one above. We were silhouetted as we stood there, praying that whoever was going to climb the stairs was on a routine check. I held on to the bar with one hand and leaned out against the grey, wet wall in an effort to avoid detection. As I did, I looked out over the city and saw the illumination of City Hall and the City Hospital. It was an exhilarating experience and to this day I can still feel the buzz.

John and I had gone over our movements and their timing hundreds of times. There were some golden rules, one of which was 'no talking'. The time allowed for this part of the plan was three minutes, which had already passed. With no sign of anyone climbing the stairs inside, I whispered to John to come up. He threw the rope up and I wrapped it around the bars in a double fashion and dropped the other end back to him, allowing him to climb up beside me. Although breaking our strict guidelines, we discussed briefly what to do. At this point I made what could have been a costly mistake. I decided to establish if we could drop down the outer wall without a rope. As I crawled towards the outer wall I noticed what appeared to be an electronic device; this caused me to stand upright, just at the point where the guards in the A and D Wing gun turrets had full view of the wall. Having stepped over the device I lowered myself to a crawl. I had to be careful that the cement debris left by the builders did not fall down and alert the guards below, who were having a bit of banter. It was a shock to see their guns and holsters as they did not wear these inside the prison. I recognised two of them. The sleet was falling in a typically slanting way and the new lights on the wall shone downwards so I reckoned that even if they did look up they would see very little, if anything. When I reached the outer wall I looked over to gauge the height, but the lights and the sleet meant I could not see the bottom.

Conscious that I was now in full view of the gun turrets to my left and right I decided to lower myself down the outside of the wall. Holding on with both hands I took another look down and reckoned that I would not survive a fall from such a height, and so decided to hoist myself back up. As I crawled back towards our anchor position at the window I had to stand up again to step over the suspicious device. Now I was really tearing up the golden rules we had set ourselves. Both John and I knew we faced a crisis, and our discussion was short and to the point. We decided to go back to the outer wall; John would hold the rope, such as it was, and I would go first; he would then drop without any aid and I would cushion his fall on the other side. It wasn't much of a plan but it was our only option. We were quietly confident, despite the unfortunate turn of events. We knew that the authorities were not yet alerted and we were now at the outer wall.

We reverted to our code of silence and when I reached the outer wall I took the end of the rope from John who was going to hold it while I dropped. We estimated that the weakened rope would still allow me about 10 feet so that I could drop the remainder without too much pain. John lay flat on the wall holding on to the rope, but as I put my faith and weight on the rope it broke, sending me down to the tarmac outside with an almighty thud. As I lay there on the flat of my back I looked upwards for John, knowing I was unable to break his fall because I could not move. I called, as loudly as I could afford, for him to jump. But when he did not appear the thought occurred that he may have fallen back inside due to the reactive force of the rope breaking. This is exactly what happened. The small consolation was that he fell into a flower bed and sustained only a broken finger, which remained disfigured for the rest of his life.

I had fallen on to cement in an area close to houses

provided for warders, which created the possibility that a warder or family member had heard the commotion. The pain was excruciating. 'If I ever get to the top of that outer wall,' I used to say, 'I will fly!' Now here I was and I couldn't even move. I leaned over on my side and managed to stand up after several attempts. But I could not walk as my heel was broken. Several times I called out in a low voice to John but received no reply. Our agreed plan allowed for every eventuality, and this was one of them. If I was the one to escape, John had given me very detailed instructions on how to proceed. A native of Belfast, he came from a committed republican family. His house could not be classed as a 'safe house'; it was regularly raided and his brother Billy had been interned without trial and imprisoned in Crumlin Road Gaol for several years while John was in A Wing. Billy was released just a few weeks before the attempted escape. Their parents, Margaret and William, were unfailing supporters of those imprisoned in Belfast jails, no matter where they came from. They supplied fruit on a weekly basis free of charge to republican prisoners over many years.

I discovered that when I stood on tiptoes I could walk, and after a last look at the top of the wall and no sign of John I decided to head towards his home, 12 Adela Street. There was no time to lose as I knew that his house would the first call the police would make when the 'balloon went up'. I was unaware of the fact that a police van from Derry had just arrived at the main prison gates, around the corner from where I was, to deliver a prisoner. Despite a broken heel, crushed cartilages in my vertebrae and a broken hand, I set off running through the large ornamental prison gates. It would be a week before I could rest again.

2

THE VIEW FROM THE OTHER SIDE

The Warders' Story

Unknown to me at the time, there was tumult in the prison as the warders checked and rechecked their numbers. Our absence from the dining hall was the subject of intense scrutiny, and our names were being called in the wing and in the recreation hall. As I ran through the streets of Belfast, Royal Ulster Constabulary (RUC) chiefs in Glenravel Street Station were being advised of the breakout. The prison Governor was called at home and given the bad news. He arrived at the prison and eventually gave the order to sound the siren, which had not been heard in Belfast since the Second World War to signal an impending air raid. The siren sounded at 5.50 p.m., just twenty minutes after we had left A Wing. I was still close to the prison when the siren wailed. The acting Chief Officer, who lived just outside the A Wing wall in one of the cottages that housed prison employees, was enjoying his St Stephen's Day evening, having finished work just an hour before. In his statement to the police he said that he immediately armed himself with his Webley revolver and ran up the side of the outer wall as far as Landscape Terrace, seeking me out. But I had just gone.

The warders' story is told in the official enquiry, ordered

by the Minister for Home Affairs. Some very interesting facts emerge from the story as told by the prison Governor and his prison officers who were on duty that night in A Wing. The first is that of a most secure prison with extraordinarily tight procedures. The second is how quickly they deduced that a breakout was in progress despite no previous recent experience (the last one had been seventeen years earlier in 1943). The third and probably the most dramatic is how little time John Kelly and I had to make our escape. It was just ten minutes – a very small window of opportunity! The details of the plan were examined very carefully, with the authorities keen to establish how we hid the electric flex and how we got hold of hacksaw blades. In general their story is very much in line with ours and, with a few exceptions, the truthfulness of their account astonished me. Although it was the most embarrassing moment of the Governor's professional career, he did not seek a scapegoat.

The enquiry begins with a report from Sir Richard Pimm, Inspector General of the RUC. (The force was replaced in 2006 by the Police Service of Northern Ireland (PSNI).) The report, sent to the Ministry of Home Affairs on 7 January 1961 (in fact Sir Richard Pimm retired that same month and was succeeded by Sir Albert Kennedy), states that one Principal Officer (PO) and six prison officers (also called warders) were 'on duty strategically stationed within the division'. It continues that at 4.15 p.m. on Monday 26 December 1960 the prisoners in A Wing were 'in association', i.e. permitted to talk and move about under supervision. At 5.40 p.m. a buzzer sounded in the area known as the Circle indicating that someone was seeking to be let out from the laundry yard. This was the yard from which we climbed on to the administration block. It states: 'Taking routine precautions to obviate an attack, the gate from the front of the laundry yard was opened and long-term "star" prisoner John Joseph Kelly was found there.' (First-time offenders serving long-term sentences were known as 'star' prisoners as the tunics they wore featured a red star on the right sleeve.) They claimed that John was of the opinion that 'Donnelly fell while endeavouring to descend to the ground outside and seemed in a grave condition'. According to the RUC, John had 'abandoned his escape attempt so that the alarm could be raised and medical help got for Donnelly'. A search of the area took place but I had gone. They found the 24-yard length of 'blanket material entwined with wire and strong cord in the laundry yard' and described the weather as being very inclement. The two guards in the gun towers had taken up duty at 4 p.m. and 5 p.m. respectively. Given the weather conditions, the report states that it was not surprising that the guards neither saw nor heard anything to arouse their suspicions.

The recently installed floodlights on the perimeter wall came in for criticism. RUC County Inspector Hopkins and District Inspector Landsdale carried out an examination two days after my escape and considered the intensity of the lighting poor. They concluded, as we had done, that 'a person moving along the escape route would not at any time come under the direct illumination in sight of the Watch Towers.' While this report was for the most part accurate, it was also self-serving as the gun towers were manned by RUC men and not by prison warders.

The exceptionally detailed and truthful report sent by Governor Lance Thompson to the Minister for Home Affairs in Stormont is probably reflective of the innate honesty of the underlying Presbyterian ethic. This report states that prisoner number 1082, D. I. Donnelly, was sentenced to ten years on 22 October 1957 for 'being and remaining a member of an unlawful organisation' and that prisoner number 4, J. J. Kelly, was given eight years for 'possessing explosive (two counts) and being a member of an unlawful organisation on 11 April 1957'. On the escape the report states:

> It is assumed that both ... crawled along the connecting wall, which is 25 feet high, with the rope and threw it over the boundary wall. The distance from where the

rope was anchored to the boundary wall is 54 feet.
Prisoner Donnelly made his escape. Prisoner Kelly states
that he heard a thud of Donnelly hitting the ground,
followed by groans. He assumed that the rope had
broken and returned to the A1 exercise yard and raised
the alarm. This was approximately 5.45 p.m.

In fact, John had fallen from the wall at the same time as I fell
on the outside. When he came to he had a serious dilemma:
raise the alarm and get medical treatment for me or assume I
had got away and just wait until discovered. He decided on a
compromise. He would allow sufficient time for me to reach
his parents' house and then raise the alarm in case I was lying
unconscious outside the walls. He need not have worried, of
course, as the warders inside A Wing had realised the two of
us were missing and his eventual alarm coincided with the
independent action of the staff to alert the RUC.

   The rest of the Governor's seven-page report gives an
account of the events of the evening and of the responsibilities of the warders. At approximately 5.30 p.m. Officer Rampf,
while patrolling A Wing, answered John Kelly's cell bell and
also unlocked Donnelly some minutes later and 'saw him
proceed to the dining hall'. Amazingly, just ten minutes later
the acting Chief Officer was alerted that there had been an
escape. The report continues:

   It was confirmed that Prisoner Donnelly had escaped.
   The alarm was sounded. This was approximately 5.50
   p.m. Most of the prison officers who were off duty and
   who lived within hearing distance of the siren answered
   the alarm very promptly and were immediately
   organised into search parties within and without the
   prison. These searches were carried on for several hours.
   District Inspectors Lansdale and Fannin and several
   members of the RUC also arrived very promptly,
   interrogated Kelly and viewed the escape route.

A quick search of John Kelly's cell revealed one hacksaw blade on the floor. Padlocks were then placed on both our empty cells. The Governor remained in the prison with the Deputy Governor until 11 p.m. and directed that every person and cell in A Wing, as well as the workshops in that division, should be thoroughly searched the following morning. In John Kelly's cell was found 'a small piece of putty which had been obviously used to conceal the cuts in the bars and window frame, four pieces of blade each approximately 5 inches long in a specially made satchel and an improvised wooden handle for a hacksaw blade. The satchel was made from clothing similar to the clothing worn by long-term star prisoners.' In Donnelly's cell, 'nothing of importance' was found. The authorities concluded that the hacksaw blade satchel was made by Donnelly who was 'employed in the tailors' workshop and had access to the necessary materials. The satchel was so made as to be easily carried inside the trousers leg.'

The detail and consideration given to every aspect of the escape is impressive. The authorities actually cut the bars and the window frame of another cell to establish how long it took. They measured the improvised rope, analysed its content and estimated the length of time it took to make. The trades officer foreman specified how the cell bars are tested and commented on the efficacy of such checks. This was in the days before standards were introduced across all industries, so in a sense the authorities in Crumlin Road Gaol were ahead of their time. In his opinion, the Governor stated, it is most difficult to detect flaws in bars and window frames. Cuts in either can be camouflaged and even tests by trades officers using hammers are not 100 per cent foolproof.

In addition to the normal daily checks by class officers, prisoners and their cells were also thoroughly searched by two officers twice a month without notice. From the report it can be seen that all spot searches were logged in the Ward Search Book showing the name of the prisoner, and the date and time of the search. This was signed by the two officers carrying out the search and countersigned both by the

Principal Officer and the Deputy Governor.

Governor Lance Thompson was rightly regarded as a martinet who ruled the prison with an iron hand. A man who never betrayed emotion, he was feared by his officers. We saw him practically every day in the prison; he stood and observed us as we walked around or sat at our benches in the workshops. There was silence when he entered a room. Known as 'the wee man' due to his small stature, he seemed to wield ultimate power over prisoners and warders alike. Despite this, however, in his report on the enquiry he shows himself to be very fair to all, although he does show his teeth when he strongly contradicts Officer Rampf's statement that it was not unusual for prisoners to be sent to the recreation hall unaccompanied: 'I cannot understand why he makes such a statement,' the Governor retorts, 'because this procedure [of always accompanying a prisoner to point of handover] is carried out equally rigidly in A Division. His statement is totally false.'

Rampf was naturally only protecting himself as he did not accompany me all the way back to the dining hall. In my own experience I would have to side with the Governor – but like all rules there are times when they are slightly bent due to circumstances. After all, there had never been even an escape attempt from A Wing in the seven years that republican prisoners were incarcerated there. Despite his anger, however, the Governor concludes his report as follows: 'I am satisfied that his [Rampf's] negligence was only the culminating point of a series of acts of omission on the part of other officers who cannot now be brought to book and I have no desire to make a scapegoat of him. I would also add that I have no reason whatsoever to suspect collusion or disloyalty on the part of any member of the prison staff.'

I believe no one was sacked because of my escape. I take a certain satisfaction in that, as all staff were conditioned to believe that an escape was impossible.

Forensic Approach

Foreman Trades Officer Tom Paisley arranged the cutting of the cell window frame and cell bars to establish how many hacksaw blades were needed and the length of time it took. His conclusions were very interesting. He found that it took a total of three hours and six minutes to cut the frame and bars, 'in unimpeded conditions'. He also surmised that it took me three hours to make the rope comprised of 'strips of 5 to 6 inch-wide blanket material laced with sisal cord at 6-inch intervals to electric cable', adding 'assuming the strips had been previously prepared'. In the rerun they used five hacksaw blades with the main difficulty being that they kept breaking long before they had lost their cutting edge. With the cell door closed, Paisley maintained that the sound of the cutting could be heard only faintly from immediately outside the door. His conclusions were generally correct, except that the noise, although not very audible from outside the door, could be clearly heard in the tier above.

Officer Rampf, from Woolwich in England, was a decent fellow. He had spent twenty-two years in the Royal Navy and had been living in Belfast since his marriage some sixteen years previously. He was almost three years in the prison service, and although a regular on A Wing initially he was seldom there in the period prior to the escape. On that day he was unlucky. Since it was a holiday, most of the regular A Wing staff were not on duty. Rampf reported to the Principal Officer and was tasked with supervising the three landings (or wards) for the hours of recreation and lock-up. Among his duties, which he began at 4.20 p.m., were to bring prisoners to the PO's office for their Christmas parcels, supervise them to their cells to leave their belongings, and return them to the dining hall. Prisoners were also allowed to go to their cells under supervision immediately after tea and before recreation commenced. When Rampf stated that it was 'not unusual for prisoners to be let out of their cells and sent down to the recreation unaccompanied and without having been passed on in A Wing', an enraged Governor questioned other warders on the issue. One claimed that 'prisoners are not permitted to go from one point to another except under supervision of an officer, either physical or visual. This is the rule of the prison and I have never known it to be relaxed.'

Rampf's statement provides a good outline of the timeline involved.

> At 5.05 p.m. the activity and movement . . . was over and the prisoners had settled down. I . . . checked all of the cells on three wards. I did A2 first and on coming to cell number 13 I found prisoners Kelly and Donnelly together. I asked Donnelly what he was doing in Kelly's cell and he stated that they were doing an Irish class together . . . I told them that there were no Irish classes that night and if they did not go down to the dining room they would be locked in their cells. Donnelly decided to go to his cell and Kelly remained in his. I satisfied myself that Kelly's cell was locked . . . I took Donnelly up and locked him in his cell. At approximately 5.30 p.m. I heard a bell being rung on A2. I went to the indicator and found it as number 13 cell, occupied by Kelly. As I unlocked his door a bell rang in A3. I told Kelly to carry on down to the dining hall and went up to A3, looked at the indicator and . . . went to this cell that was occupied by Donnelly. He stated that he wanted to go to the A1 dining hall . . . I saw him go down the flight of stairs. At about 5.35 I went down to check the numbers with the prison officer on duty and he stated that he had sixty-nine in the dining hall. I said to him 'you should have seventy-one' . . . I asked him if Donnelly and Kelly had come to him. He said Kelly had not come but he couldn't place Donnelly just then. I went straight to the Principal Officer and told him that I could not account for two prisoners.

In the intervening couple of minutes Rampf heard someone

say: 'There is [sic] two men out in the yard.' He states that he went straight to Kelly's cell and immediately saw that some of the window bars and window grille had been cut out and removed. He also saw a hacksaw blade sticking out of a cardboard box below the window. As he locked the cell door, the chief officer arrived and ordered a thorough check to be made of everyone. Rampf's statement to Head Constable Millar on 27 December finishes with this comment: 'I did not consider it peculiar that they should elect to be locked in their own cells and that both almost at the same time – about twenty-five minutes later – should ring their bells to go to recreation.'

Rampf should not have been too displeased with the performance of his duties as he let me out of the cell at 5.30 p.m. and just five minutes later knew that something was wrong. Until I read this report I always imagined that we had much more time. Time seems to have passed in slow motion.

An unnamed officer told Head Constable Millar that he was ordered to get the prisoners out of the dining hall at 5.50 p.m. and lock them in their cells. He was not told why but complied immediately. 'After all prisoners had been locked up I assisted in checking the cells in A3 with another officer. I noticed that one cell, I believe number 10, was unoccupied and I pointed this to another warder who informed me that two prisoners had escaped and the occupant of the cell, Donnelly, was one of them.'

Another unnamed warder stated:

> I took up duty as armed guard between the inner gates at the main entrance to the prison. The three main gates are kept locked from 4.20 p.m. on holidays ... I hold the keys of the two inner gates, the key to the grille gate leading to the officers' quarters off the main entrance and also a key to the laundry yard or recreation ground of A Division. Another [armed] officer was the gate officer on the front main gate. I only leave my post between the two inner gates when necessary to unlock the gate

leading to A Division recreation yard which is 20 yards from my post in order to facilitate police in and out of the yard between the watch towers, which is once every hour or so. In my position between the inner gates I had a limited view of the high wall running from the south of the administration block to the west front of the entrance building. On the night of 26 December 1960 it was sleeting and snowing.

He finishes his statement by saying that he was part of a group that searched the outside area as far as Landscape Terrace. He reveals that at 5.35 p.m. a police van called at the prison. 'It did not drive inside, but two policemen deposited a prisoner inside the main gate. The police did not go beyond the first gate and the prisoner was taken by a Principal Officer.' This was just about the time I was lying in a heap around the corner from them. I would have been very unlucky to have been discovered by the random delivery of a prisoner by two policemen from Derry on a most unusual day and time.

The Principal Officer in charge of A Wing that night was John Foster, 6 foot 4 in height. He was known among his peers as 'John the Fox' due to his cuteness. He was not easily fooled and some of his subordinates had fallen foul of his authority because they underestimated him. He served twelve years in the British Army and had previously been a bus conductor in Derry. He joined the prison service in 1947 and had worked in Derry Gaol before Crumlin Road. In 1958 he was promoted to Principal Officer. Very much the professional, he was always active around the wing when on duty. Almost always in good humour, he knew the prison like the back of his hand, having served in every wing during the previous twelve years. His job that night was to allocate specific duties to the officers under his charge and to supervise them. This was mostly done by issuing orders and taking interim reports from the various warders as they kept him up to date with what was happening.

In his signed statement to Detective Sergeant Whiteside

he sets out his recollection of events.

> At 5.40 p.m. an officer [Rampf] reported to me that he was in doubt about two star class prisoners, he not having been able to account for them. As I was about to investigate I got a sudden call from the Principal Officer who was in charge of the rest of the prison that two prisoners were in the laundry yard. I immediately ran and entered the laundry yard and as I did so I saw John Joseph Kelly, a star class prisoner, standing just inside the gate dressed in his shirt and trousers. On taking Kelly to lock him in a cell he told me to hurry and get the other fellow as he was badly injured. Kelly did not name the other prisoner. I did hurry and locked Kelly in a cell in C Division and rushed around the extern wall at the rear of the prison cottages. On seeing the other Principal Officer ahead of me I returned to the prison and made a thorough search of the laundry yard and ball alley. By this time the Governor and police had arrived. All prisoners were returned to their cells and a thorough check was made of the division and it was discovered that long-term star prisoner Donnelly was missing.

Political Fallout and Media Coverage

The newspapers gave the escape headlines for several days and much of the reporting was similar to the *Daily Express* report on 28 December 1960: 'As 12,000 Ulster Police and B Specials began one of the biggest manhunts an enquiry was being held in Belfast Jail into the amazing escape. The escape is all the more remarkable because it is vaunted as the most stringently guarded jail in the British Isles. Searchlights play up and down the walls from watch towers manned by guards with machine guns.'

In February 1961 Unionist MP Nat Minford alluded to the escape in the Stormont parliament.

In the newspapers last Sunday I noticed that . . . Daniel Donnelly who is now in Cork gave an interview to the press about how he escaped. He actually boasted about it . . . He and Kelly climbed out through the window and by devious methods got to the outer wall. He climbed out and fortunately the rope broke. It seems incredible to me that at the time of the escape anyone could have got out of Crumlin Road Gaol so easily as this person seems to have done. It seems to me incredible that the steel bars of a window could be filed through and yet remain unnoticed; that two men could creep across the top of walls in between searchlights and not be seen by the men at the gun posts; that one of them could escape and find refuge in Belfast and four days later land in Cork.

Nat Minford expressed the concern of most unionists, but for nationalists it was a great boost.

Brian Faulkner was Minister for Home Affairs at the time, and would later become Northern Ireland Prime Minister. Faulkner claimed that for security reasons no details of the escape would be made public. He was protective of the authorities and claimed the weather conditions on the night aided the breakout. 'The Hon. Member for Antrim mentioned that it seemed hard to understand why the police guards who are posted on the exterior walls of the prison failed to notice this escape. I would suggest that the weather handicapped those police guards considerably in exercising their vigilance from their watch towers on the prison walls.' Faulkner also quashed rumours that prison employees aided the escape in any way. 'In my opinion the one redeeming feature of the whole thing is that following a full enquiry into the episode there is absolutely no suggestion whatsoever of either collusion or disloyalty of any member or members of the prison staff.'

The breakout was front-page news when the papers reappeared a few days later following the holiday period. Although much of the information was accurate, a lot was completely untrue. In its February 1961 issue the republican monthly, the *United Irishman*, focused on the search for the escapee.

> The escape touched off the most extensive manhunt ever known in the occupied area. Activity of Crown forces was particularly intense on all roads leading from Derry to Donegal. On Craigavon Bridge in Derry a permanent roadblock was set up and sustained for days. Belfast and district were enclosed in a ring of steel from 6 p.m. on December 26th. Squads of heavily armed RUC and B Specials aided by Special Branch 'experts' descended on known republican houses. Some were raided again and again in the days that followed. Among those singled out for particular attention were recently released republican prisoners. Right into the New Year and throughout the first week the huge manhunt continued without rest. Rumour was rife. The escapee was in the United States – he was here, he was there, he was everywhere and nowhere as far as the British occupying forces were concerned.

All papers carried the following statement from the Irish Republican Publicity Bureau issued on 8 January 1961. 'On the evening of December 26th 1960 two Irish Republican Prisoners serving sentences of penal servitude made a bid for freedom. One of them, John Kelly of Belfast, did not succeed. The other, Daniel Donnelly of Omagh, County Tyrone, has now reported back to the Republican Movement and is in safe hands.'

The *Belfast Telegraph* attempted to second-guess my movements following the escape.

> Donnelly dropped behind houses where a family was having its evening meal – there the trail ends. In the prison houses children were playing with their toys they got the day before when Donnelly, still dressed in his grey prison garb with a red star on his arm, crept past.

When he dropped over the wall he is thought to have turned right through the gate near the Masonic Hall on which there is not normally a police guard. Had he turned left he would have had to pass the illuminated gate of the prison on which there is a guard.

In February the *Telegraph* carried a provocative piece about extradition. Seán Lemass had become Taoiseach in the South and the paper speculated on whether he would hand over persons wanted by the authorities in the North. 'In any steps he may take the case of Daniel Donnelly who escaped from Crumlin Road Gaol will be examined. Apart from the political nature of his offences Donnelly, as a convicted criminal, is in a different category to others on the run.' The *United Irishman*, meanwhile, had its own take on the issue. 'Mr Lemass is trying hard, we know, but he will surely find it difficult to satisfy the unceasing demands of the British garrison in Ireland, and the Irish people have a thing or two to say in the matter, remember.'

The nationalist *Irish News* told of the authorities' reaction following the breakout. 'People in the east end of the city first became aware that something extraordinary had happened when they heard three loud explosions accompanied by bright flares. They were the alarm signals set off at the new police headquarters at Ladas Drive near Castlereagh.'

The paper also speculated on my movements once outside the prison walls. 'It has not yet been established whether Donnelly had an accomplice or accomplices outside with a waiting car, but it is considered likely that this was the case. The route he took again illustrates that the escape was meticulously planned as on it he was least likely to be confronted by guards or other security precautions.'

On New Year's Day the *Sunday Independent* had an interesting story.

Daniel Ignatius Donnelly . . . was reported last night to have reached New York by air from Shannon. The report came from republican sources in Belfast and it is stated that he flew from Shannon within two days of his escape . . . It was known that Donnelly may have been free for anything up to two hours before the alarm was raised in the prison. In that time, if he had outside help and transport had been laid on, he could have been well over the border before the police dragnet became effective. But the police are still not convinced that Donnelly has left Belfast. They think that he may be ready to make a break from the city within the next few days and the police alert is being maintained at full pressure.

The English *Daily Mail* reported that 'Daniel Donnelly walked boldly through an unguarded gate and was whisked away in a car by accomplices. The escape was planned for months. Donnelly sawed the bars in his cell window. Particles of dust were hidden or carried out in his pocket to the exercise yard for disposal.'

The now defunct *Irish Press* quoted an RUC spokesman as saying, 'We are convinced that he is still in the city. We have every road covered and it would be impossible for him to get out', while *The Irish Times* reported: 'Police were on guard at Nutts Corner watching all persons who boarded planes leaving the airport. The boats for Britain were intensively scrutinised. Special Constables were called out all over Northern Ireland and RUC called back to duty. There were special police patrols in the area of the prison as it is thought that Donnelly might have gone to a hideout near the prison prepared for possible escapees.' The following day the paper reported: 'The police believe that Donnelly is being treated for his injuries somewhere in Belfast.'

The Omagh-based *Ulster Herald* gave some background information on the local boy. 'Young Donnelly, known to his friends as Danny, is one of the sons of Mr Peter Donnelly, a retired railway official, and Mrs Donnelly and while in prison had been studying for a university degree having taken his matriculation last year with high distinction. Young Donnelly

... escaped in a manner that recalled Red Hugh O'Donnell's Christmas breakout from Dublin Castle centuries ago.'

Another Tyrone paper, the *Dungannon Observer*, was absolutely thrilled with the escape; its headlines included 'How did he do it?' and 'The invisible man'. The paper reported that:

> Mid-Ulster Unionists were shocked at the ease with which Donnelly escaped. 'Is this the kind of return we are getting for all the money that is being spent on security?' one man asked. A similar question was heard being put to a policeman in charge of a patrol on the Lisburn–Belfast Road shortly after five o'clock on Tuesday morning. The policeman, obviously embarrassed by this question, replied that everything was being done that could be done. He agreed that Donnelly would need to be as elusive as a Lough Neagh eel to get through the police cordon that had been thrown up around the city of Belfast.

3

IT'S IN THE BLOOD

Three years and two months earlier, in October 1957, Northern Ireland Lord Chief Justice McDermott sentenced me to ten years in prison on the single charge of membership of the Irish Republican Army (IRA), a proscribed organisation under the Special Powers Act of Northern Ireland. It was a charge the authorities only used when all else failed as they had no wish to enable republican prisoners to seek prisoner of war status. Very few political prisoners in A Wing were charged with such membership even though they may have proclaimed their affiliation. The Stormont government preferred to treat all prisoners charged with political offences as criminals, which was how we were treated in the 1950s. Internees who were imprisoned without trial from 1956 to 1962 were afforded political status – they could wear their own clothes, have food parcels sent in, have free association and were not obliged to work. We had to wear a grey uniform of tunic-type jacket with a red star on the right sleeve, trousers, shirt, thick socks and boots.

I was tried in Belfast and was arraigned with nine other Tyrone men who were charged with blowing up drill halls and forming-up centres for the B Specials. The halls were in Beragh, Eskra, Skelga and Fintona. We were also charged with conspiracy to cause these explosions, but this charge was dropped in January 1958, as conspiracy is a difficult charge to prove. It was, however, used as a legal device so that when each individual was being sentenced the book of evidence could be applied to all. This aspect was not challenged legally so it made it easy for the prosecution to achieve their ends.

It was the practice of the IRA at the time to refuse to recognise the jurisdiction of the Northern Ireland Courts. I refused to recognise the right of the Court or Lord Chief Justice McDermott to try me and so a jury was in place, and it took ten minutes to find me guilty. A pupil at the Christian Brothers-run Mount St Columba School in Omagh, I was seventeen when arrested in the summer of 1957.

Lord Chief Justice McDermott made a real sabre-rattling speech when sentencing us, referring to the possibility of introducing the death penalty for such offences. Nine men from the Omagh area were sentenced to various terms of imprisonment that day. Fergus McCabe, Tattyreagh, Frank Cullen, Corbo, Clogher, Arthur McCarroll, Eskra and Hugh Darcy, Tattyreagh received four years each; Jim Darcy, Tattyreagh and Patrick Devlin, Seskinore received five years, Jim Devlin, Edergole, six and Seán McHugh, Donaghanie, Beragh, eight years. James Gallagher, a 42-year-old Fermanagh man who had come to live in Omagh some years earlier, was charged with conspiracy and was held on remand until January 1958. The charge was dropped and he was interned without trial for six years.

My own family tradition for generations had been radical and republican. My granduncle Michael Gallagher, also known as 'Red Mick', served six years in Crumlin Road from 1936 when with twelve others he was charged with felony after being arrested in Belfast. A member of the IRA Army Council for a time in the 1930s, 'Red Mick' was a farmer who lived in Correshkin near Dromore in County Tyrone. That particular trial was a travesty of justice and the records show that there was no real evidence. Among the thirteen were some of the highest ranking northern IRA men gathered at Crown Entry in the centre of Belfast to hold a court martial. An informer had tipped off the RUC, and all present were arrested when a large force of police raided the premises.

The subsequent court case heard that where the arrests were made was a copy of a republican publication called *An Síol*, the content of which, the Crown insisted, constituted incitement. After fifty minutes the unionist jury found all guilty. The names read like a 'who's who' of Irish republicanism in the 1930s. James Killeen from Dublin, later the head of the National Cycling Association which had both an athletic and a political agenda, was sentenced under the alias James Grace. Seán McCool from Stranorlar, James Steel, the Belfast man who later escaped from Crumlin Road with Hugh McAteer in 1943, and Michael Traynor, from Belfast, later to become treasurer of Sinn Féin in the 1950s, were also jailed. Charlie McGlade, prominent in the provisional movement during the 1970s and 1980s, was one of the youngest. The others were less well known: John McNally, William James Rice and William Mulholland, all from Belfast; John Collins Fox from Obin Street, Portadown; John McAdam from the Bogside, Derry and Michael O'Boyle from Belvedere Place, Dublin, whose real name was Michael A. Kelly. This all happened three years before I was born but fate decreed that I would meet a number of these men in the years ahead.

The nephew of the man who prosecuted Uncle Mick prosecuted me. Michael Traynor was a regular visitor to Omagh during the Mid-Ulster election campaigns of 1955 and I met him often at that time. He was then living in Dublin where he owned a tailoring business. Charlie McGlade's brother Frank was detained in prison when I was there. Charlie came to live in Dublin also and was a well-known and most likeable man whom I met often. Uncle Mick had been sentenced to three years in July 1922 for IRA activity and was described at the time as 'one of the most dangerous members of the IRA in Northern Ireland'. The B men raided his house and, according to Mick's wife, stole money and gold sovereigns. She wrote to Michael Collins, who in turn wrote to Sir James Craig, the first prime minister of Northern Ireland, complaining of such harassment. In his reply Sir James rejected the charge. To think that those two great personalities were corresponding about an event in a townland in County Tyrone! It recalls Patrick Kavanagh's lines of how Homer 'made the Iliad of such a local row. Gods make their own importance'.

On the occasion of King George V's silver jubilee in May 1935 Mick extinguished a bonfire lit by some unionist neighbours, and in the process pushed a couple of people who attempted to stop him. This was later turned into a charge of 'assaulting two women', for which he received four months. Mick's experience in the Crown Entry case made him wary of being involved with republican projects for the rest of his life.

When I came to Dublin in 1963 I met Maurice Twomey, IRA Chief of Staff in the 1930s. I was in his very attractive craft and souvenir shop on O'Connell Street, having no idea who the owner was, when on hearing my accent he engaged me in conversation and within seconds was talking animatedly about the courage and feats of 'Red' Mick Gallagher.

Stories of Mick's exploits were told many times. We loved to meet him but he seldom spoke of his activities.

My father's brother, Frank Donnelly, spent time in Derry Gaol, also in the 1940s, for IRA activity. He later emigrated to Canada and died there a single man in 1953. He and another uncle, Paddy, were part of an IRA unit in Tyrone who did what they could to keep the separatist spirit alive at a time of few civil rights for Catholics in the Six Counties.

My father's eldest brother, Michael Donnelly, was a courier for John Devoy, the Irish-American Fenian. Michael travelled the world on board liners, usually as a steward. A literary and artistic man, he was friendly with Countess Markievicz, the Plunketts and the Giffords and many of the other 1916 families. He was also an actor and featured in one of the first silent films ever made in Ireland – *Knocknagow: The*

Homes of Tipperary. The original story was written by the Fenian, Charles Kickham.

Madame Czira, a sister of Grace Gifford who was famed in song and story as the bride of Joseph Mary Plunkett on the eve of his execution by the British in Kilmainham Gaol in May 1916, told me that my uncle Michael had done tremendous work for the Rising and in preparation for the War of Independence. I met her in 1971 at a garden party attended also by Fiona Plunkett, sister of Joseph Mary Plunkett. Madame Czira wrote columns for newspapers under the pseudonym 'John Brennan' since it was difficult in those days for a woman to have articles published. She wrote that on one occasion Michael was presumed dead as a result of a liner being sunk by the Germans during the First World War. His republican friends organised a requiem mass for him in St Francis Xavier's Church in Sherrard Street, Dublin, which was packed on the day. Some weeks later, however, Michael walked in to one of their Sunday morning gatherings. He had been on a different liner. Uncle Mickey, as we affectionately called him, was an important resource for the republican cause for a long period. He died accidentally of gas poisoning in Philadelphia in 1923, just thirty years old.

Michael had taken the republican side in the Civil War (1922–3) and therefore had broken off relations with John Devoy, who supported the 1921 Treaty that set up the Irish Free State and surrendered the six counties of Tyrone, Fermanagh, Derry, Armagh, Down and Antrim to the British. In later years I had the opportunity of seeing the Knocknagow film. It was a strange experience – one that tape recorders and old film reels can evoke – seeing and hearing the voice of someone long dead and yet whose name is part of a person's family or social history. It was unforgettable. As the camera came in for a close-up he smiled slightly, confirming his identity to us because, in appearance, he was so like our uncle Jim who worked in the post office in Omagh.

Granny Donnelly, older sister of 'Red Mick', opened a

restaurant in George's Street in Omagh near the Catholic
Sacred Heart Church. Called 'The Tyrone Restaurant', it
became one of the best-known and best-liked eating houses
in the west of the county. Its two large dining areas, one
upstairs and the other downstairs, became regular meeting
rooms. When just a small boy I saw Éamon de Valera, Seán
MacBride, Alex Donnelly and many others in the restaurant
taking part in Anti-Partition League meetings, which were
held during the 1940s all over the Six Counties. In later years,
following the successful election of anti-partitionists Anthony
Mulvey and Paddy Cunningham to Westminster as
abstentionist MPs, we believed that Tyrone and Fermanagh
were on the brink of being given back to the Free State.

Donnelly's restaurant was the nerve centre for election
activities. In those days the GAA were banned from flying the
Irish Tricolour even in their own playing field, and on one
occasion my grandmother, an unrepentant Fenian, carried the
flag in front of a parade and led it down through the main
street of the town to the GAA pitch, despite threats from the
RUC.

Crumlin Road Gaol

On 22 October 1957 I was brought through the dark, damp
and smelly tunnel that connects Crumlin Road Courthouse to
the prison. The previous month I had 'celebrated' my
eighteenth birthday. Staying in prison until I was twenty-eight
was not in my plans. I remember well the feeling of despair as
we trudged through the tunnel accompanied by many
warders. We were all shocked at the severity of the sentences
and the venom of the Lord Chief Justice. The longest sentence
for IRA membership up until then had been two years.
Having refused to recognise the right of the puppet Stormont
government to try me as an Irishman I had no redress but to
plan my escape. I started that very day.

Crumlin Road Gaol – or Belfast Prison as it was also
called – was a cold, forbidding building with all the hallmarks

of a dungeon. Built between 1843 and 1845 it had four wings named A, B, C and D and 640 cells. B Wing was retained for short-term prisoners serving two years or less and also juvenile offenders. C Wing was reserved for prisoners on remand awaiting trial and detainees, while D Wing housed internees, political prisoners against whom no evidence existed but whom the authorities considered a threat to the state. Men were kept there only on suspicion and their imprisonment authorised by the signature of the Minster for Home Affairs. Some were kept there from December 1956 to 1962.

The Circle was the nerve centre of the prison. There were several locked gates between each wing and the Circle to ensure the highest security and to prevent warders being taken hostage. The Circle led into the administration block which formed the front part of the whole complex and housed the offices, visiting rooms, Governor's office and, upstairs, the chapel or common room. In front of this block was a quadrangle directly in front of the main gates with their armed guards. The entire prison was encircled by a 25-foot-high wall, higher in some places.

The cells were 12 feet by 7 feet and 10 feet high. In my first cell there was a concave valley in the centre of the floor, several inches deep, caused by men walking up and down over many years. It was a constant reminder of the tragic lives lived by generations of men who, rightly or wrongly, found themselves in this horrific place. The very thick cell door was recessed and made from hard steel with two small apertures sealed with transparent strong glass. The furniture in the cell was sparse. There was a single bed made of steel with a wire base and a mattress, pillow, two sheets and two blankets. There was a wooden chair, a small table and a cupboard with two shelves for the few personal belongings that a prisoner might have. A metal pipe ran through the cells, bringing some heat in winter. Occasionally prisoners used the pipe as a communication conduit, usually by a pre-arranged knocking code. There was also a mirror on the wall to allow for shaving.

The uncovered light bulb in the centre of the ceiling was operated from outside the cell by the warders. In the corner behind the door was the 'po' or chamber pot.

Each cell had a window measuring about 3 feet by 2 feet. It had four vertical and two horizontal bars made from solid steel. Then there was a metal frame with small panes of glass integrated – seven across and three down. Two were without glass to allow air circulation. These had to be stuffed with newspapers during wet or cold nights, but the paper had to be removed every morning by order of the prison authorities. The metal frame was cemented into the wall of the window at an angle; there was an attached metal lid which had about 4 inches of movement to allow it to be closed in cold weather or to remain open to allow fresh air when required. The metal frame also acted as an additional security barrier.

Cells were on each side of the corridor, and on three floors. At the end of each level there was a toilet, and a sluice cell for the emptying of chamber pots. Most of the wings had one large cell on each floor to allow for three prisoners; these usually housed the orderlies – prisoners who helped to implement the 'slop out' at the start of the day, brought up the food from the cookhouse and cleaned the floors of the wings. A Wing had three common dining rooms on each level; in the evening these served as recreation rooms where prisoners could play cards, table tennis or billiards. A Wing had its own entry through A3 to the chapel or common room. On the ground floor of A Wing were two doors that led out to the yards. The Crumlin Road side featured a pleasant lawn and garden with some flower beds and a perimeter path for strolling. Political prisoners and first-time offenders were allowed to walk around the yard for one hour on Monday, Wednesday and Friday morning and for recreation on summer evenings. The other prisoners used that yard on alternate days, when we used 'the football yard' on the other side. We were counted in and out of the yards one by one, with the warders keeping constant watch.

The tunnel to the courthouse could be seen from the garden yard. I remember particularly Kevin Mallon and Francie Talbot, who were charged with the murder of RUC Sergeant Ovens in Coalisland, walking through when we were there. There were very strong rumours that they had been badly beaten by the police. They were acquitted of the charge but sentenced for arms offences and joined us in A Wing in 1958.

This yard also housed the workshops – the laundry, the tailors and the cobblers – which could only be accessed through an internal corridor beside the A Wing dining room, and a shed for prisoners to take shelter in wet weather. One side of the administration block looked out onto this yard, so the Governor could peer out his office window and see us as we walked around in pairs. There was a window on the second floor behind which, it was rumoured, armed guards were ready in the event of any attempted breakout or an attack from outside.

From my first day in Crumlin Road I intended to escape. In later years Dan Moore from Newry, with whom I had been detained for several weeks, told me that on hearing of my escape he said, 'I bet you Donnelly went through the front gate – he always said that's how he would do it.' Escaping, however, proved a lot more difficult than I thought. Drawing up a viable plan would take me three years as so many things had to be taken into consideration. But ironically it was the authorities who gave the greatest assistance when they raised the height of the inner link wall.

4

EARLY YEARS

I was born on 8 September 1939, the youngest of six boys, to Peter and Margaret Donnelly (née Doherty) in a part of Omagh known colloquially as 'Gallows Hill'. My mother often reminded me over the years that I shared a birthday with the Blessed Virgin Mary. My brothers and I spent our summer holidays from school in our Granny Doherty's house, named 'Grouse Park', on a small farm at the foot of the mountain Bessy Belle near Newtownstewart. I remember something strange happening every year during the marching season around the twelfth of July when our Protestant neighbours, for a short period of time, kept to themselves. I learned in later years that this was due to an Orange Lodge rule that forbade Orangemen from unnecessary fraternising with Catholics. It was permissible to work and chat with Catholics but to go to their houses at night was disapproved of as 'unnecessary fraternising'.

Our terrace on Gallows Hill had five houses. We occupied the first and my mother's younger sister and her family (the Devines) lived in the last. So the occupants of the first and last houses were Catholics while the middle three were Protestants. Relations were extremely good. Although primarily a Catholic (nationalist) area, Gallows Hill also housed a number of Protestant families. Many of my friends were Protestant; they attended the Model School and later the Omagh Academy or the Technical School while we went to the Christian Brothers' Primary School and later the Brothers' Grammar School.

Our next door neighbours were the Kinloughs, with whom we were on very good terms. When I was in Crumlin Road Mrs Kinlough came to visit me with my mother, an extraordinarily courageous thing to do in those years. In return I had a linen handkerchief painted with the outline of a Union Jack and 'King Billy' on his white horse jumping through it. I framed it and sent it to the Kinloughs as a Christmas present. Other neighbours would press a couple of half crowns and occasionally a 10 shilling note into my mother's hand with the whispered message 'buy something for Danny'. Gallows Hill was a real community. Families lived in close proximity and children were expected to obey their elders – no matter who they were. Neighbours looked out for one another in the very difficult war years and after. Borrowing a cup of sugar was a common occurrence and that image is often used now to express the intimacy and respect that a genuine community reflects.

The Christian Brothers provided our family's education. In my time the Brothers dressed in black soutane with a sash and a white collar that was narrower than that worn by priests. They took vows of poverty, chastity and obedience, and their monthly pay was returned to the Order for the building and maintenance of schools. These men lived on a weekly stipend that bought them a couple of packets of cigarettes which was, for most of them, their only 'vice'. They were amazing men with an extraordinary commitment. They were mostly intellectuals who guided, encouraged and supported the ordinary people and their children. Their love of the Irish language and their spirited nationalism meant that they were often blamed for creating rebels, and indeed they did teach history with a certain emphasis on the underdog. In my primary school approximately half the staff were lay teachers while the other half were Brothers, but in the grammar (formerly called secondary) school the balance was more towards lay teachers. The Brothers came from all over the country and we loved to mimic their accents.

Brother O'Connell from Limerick was a great favourite

with the boys, as he played handball and organised athletics. Brother O'Byrne from Wexford was a huge GAA fan and indeed the O'Byrne Cup is named after his late father. Brother McQuillan was another Gaelic football and hurling fan and attended all of the local matches. Brother Hamill from Belfast was a marvellous choirmaster and his charges won cups and medals at all the Feiseanna. He visited many houses on 'The Hill' on Christmas morning and could be seen with his rolled umbrella and quick gait as he scurried around. Having spent time in China he was a constant promoter of the Columban Missions. His brother Mickey Hamill was a famous soccer player and has been described as the George Best of his day. Mickey played for Glasgow Celtic, Manchester United, Manchester City and, of course, Belfast Celtic. The English media of the time described him as the world's greatest centre half. He died tragically and his body was taken from the river Lagan in July 1943. Our parents talked a lot about Mickey's football talents and this gave his brother, our Brother Hamill, a certain celebrity status.

Brother Tom Nagle, who is buried in Omagh's Dublin Road Graveyard, was a Corkman and an expert in the Irish language. He was also a dedicated gardener and encouraged an understanding and respect for the environment before it became popular. The autumn leaves that covered the schoolyard were gathered and used as compost. He was the original green environmentalist.

Brother McGee was from Kerry and taught me in my last year at grammar school. Well over 6 feet tall with a mane of white hair, he instilled in me an understanding and appreciation of English poetry and literature. How I appreciated that enlightenment in my prison cell. I could 'escape' out the window as I read good literature by Iris Murdoch or the poetry of Yeats and Milton. On his first day Brother McGee launched into a ballad sometimes recited by the actor Harry Brogan on RTÉ's *The Walton's Programme*. It was the tragic love story of a trapeze artist. Brother McGee held us spellbound, and when he finished he asked us to maintain that interest while he read Keats' 'Ode to a Grecian Urn'. I was captivated.

Brother Murphy from Wexford was the superior after Brother Ryan. A marvellous coach and careers guidance adviser, he also had a great love of music and organised many excellent Christian Brothers Concerts in Omagh's Town Hall. All of the teachers took on a number of entertainment projects and many of Omagh's best loved singers had their first opportunity on the Town Hall stage with the Brothers. I have a special affection for Brother Murphy. He came twice to Crumlin Road to visit me, a daunting experience for anyone at that time. He was delayed in the waiting room for hours, was subjected to searches and generally made to feel unwelcome. Then he had the indignity of having to speak to me with a warder sitting between us at a table.

None of the priests of the parish ever visited me even though I had been an active member of the Legion of Mary and an altar boy for several years. Mind you, it would have been very awkward for them, as the bishops had denounced Operation Harvest and deemed that support for the campaign constituted a mortal sin. Visits were restricted to one per month, and it was usually family members who came. Special permits could be sought but were not always granted. At Brother Murphy's funeral many years later I had the great privilege of being asked by his family to say a few words at the graveside. I paid tribute with a quotation from the former Cork Lord Mayor Terence MacSwiney: 'He has led a beautiful life, he has left a beautiful field, he has sacrificed the hour to give service forever, he has gone to join the great with whom he will be honoured forever.'

Generations of children in Omagh were educated to a high standard by the Christian Brothers and the Loreto nuns, both of whom are owed a great debt by the people of Ireland for their unselfish undertaking in providing free education well before it became government policy.

Unionist Hegemony

The Stormont government despised the fact that the Catholic Church had insisted on a separate education for their people. There were two issues here: one was the religious ethos that underlay all Catholic education while the second was the fact that that section of the population loosely described as 'nationalist' did not want their children brought up as 'little Englanders' with the Union Jack as their flag. The Stormont regime showed its displeasure by restricting grants for the building of Catholic schools to 65 per cent, necessitating fund-raising events to meet the shortfall. This situation was talked about daily as we grew up, so there was a constant sense of unfairness. Even the Mater Hospital in Belfast used the football pools, which cost a shilling a week, to help pay for new equipment. It was a mean-spirited, uncaring and eventually damaging policy. It informed our view of the British-imposed government and it was not a good one.

Then during my formative years there were occasional local political scandals where the best houses were allotted to Protestants. Omagh town was over 60 per cent Catholic and, politically speaking therefore, mostly Nationalist. Despite this, we grew up with a Unionist-controlled Omagh Urban Council. This was achieved in two ways: first, there was the 'property vote', which allowed those who paid rates to the council to have multiple votes. Protestants were the owners of most property and businesses in the town and so unionism benefited directly from this qualification; second, there was the policy of 'gerrymandering'. The town was broken up into areas and a certain number of elected representatives assigned to each of them. These areas were very cunningly constructed to allow for those with a Catholic majority to be clumped together with a lesser number of elected representatives assigned to them and then, where the authorities wished to have Unionist councillors, they would include a substantial minority of Catholics in the knowledge that they were not enough to upset the final vote. Elections were run on a 'first

past the post' basis, unlike in the South which adopted
proportional representation (PR). The result was a comfortable
majority of Unionists controlling the affairs of Omagh even
though they actually represented only 39 per cent of the
population. The governance of the town was therefore totally
biased in favour of the unionist (Protestant) community. But
it had not always been like that. After the Redistribution of
Seats (Ireland) Act of 1918 Omagh had a town council based
on universal suffrage and one that reflected the composition of
the electorate, up until 1928 when new constituencies were
established. This explains why the name plates on many streets
– such as Ardán Naomh Pádraig on 'The Hill' and Ascal
Naomh Mhiceál, Brookmount – are still to be seen in the
town in the old Gaelic script.

Unionist dominance manifested itself in the allocation of
jobs on the council, in administration and among manual
workers. The mandatory flying of the Union Jack on the Town
Hall and Courthouse was a constant source of annoyance to
nationalists. It also exposed the lack of any understanding of
fairness in the council's treatment of the majority. On one
famous occasion BBC Northern Ireland were recording a
programme about Omagh and its hinterland with an emphasis
on personalities. They invited the poetess Alice Milligan who,
although a practising Presbyterian, was a republican and
supporter of the 1916 Rising. Alice waited for the programme
makers' call at her great friend Denis Flanagan's house across
the road from the Town Hall. While having tea, the runner for
the programme would come at regular intervals and say 'One
hour now, Miss Milligan' and then several more times until
'Five minutes now, Miss Milligan.' Alice called him at the last
moment and said in her very authoritarian manner, 'I could
not possibly enter that building until that flag has been
removed.' Her timing was spot on. The BBC needed her on
the programme and with no negotiating time left, the flag was
hauled down. Not for the first time the name of Alice Milligan
entered the folklore of Omagh.

The 1951 Flags and Emblems Bill banned any flags, badges or bunting that purported to represent an expression of Irish nationalism. This made criminals of us, not because of what we had done but because of who we were. The Stormont government was hugely paranoid about any attempt by Catholics to celebrate their nationality. Their own culture had the full run of the streets and roads of the town; there seemed to be Orange parades for every season, not just July. I remember as a boy going with some of my Protestant friends to Campsie (Omagh) in November to hear the pipe bands play while the effigy of Robert Lundy was burned. (My mother was not pleased when she heard where I had been.) Lundy was one of the Apprentice Boys defenders in Derry in 1690 and had attempted to open the gates of the city to the Catholic King James. He was regarded as a traitor by the unionists and the term 'Lundy' to denote such a person became popular. So there were Orange parades, Black Preceptory parades and Apprentice Boys parades, and they also used the same bands and many of the same banners to commemorate the Battle of the Somme in 1916 in which many soldiers from all over Ireland, both Catholic and Protestant, died.

All this gave us the sense of being strangers in our own country. Growing up in Omagh there was no way of avoiding the widespread discrimination. Catholics had no chance of a job in the town or county council and certainly not as civil servants. While some Catholics were so employed, the numbers were minuscule. The Six Counties, as we always called it, was an artificial set-up. The boundary of the state was drawn in such a way as to create a permanent majority for those who considered themselves British. The high birth rate among Catholics caused some panic, so the authorities decided that jobs would be given to Protestants only, with just a token Catholic here and there. Those Catholics who found themselves on the dole were then pressurised into emigration. In 1961 some 56 per cent of emigrants were Catholic while they made up just 38 per cent of the population. In my own house my brother Peadar went to Canada in 1952 followed by Gerry (who later returned to Omagh), Eugene went to Birmingham where he spent most of his life, Kevin to Scotland and Jim to Canada and eventually to Cambridge, England – and I went to prison. Apart from the last named, this was a common story among Catholics. The number of jobs available to them in the higher echelons of the civil service, police or local government was practically nil.

The situation eventually led to the Civil Rights campaign in the late 1960s for 'one man, one vote'. The structure of Omagh Urban Council was a constant reminder of the injustices perpetrated against Catholics. The Civil Rights campaign banished the word 'gerrymandering' from everyday use when universal franchise was eventually granted to the Six Counties. Omagh had been divided into three wards with a designated number of representatives assigned to each: North (6), South (6) and West (9). The first two had an artificially created majority of unionist voters while the latter had a large majority of nationalists. This effectively led to a permanent Unionist majority. The malign success of these measures can best be judged by the fact that when gerrymandering was eventually brought to an end by the McCrory Report in 1973 and PR introduced, fifteen Nationalist councillors were elected to Omagh District Council out of a total of twenty-one.

We grew up in an atmosphere of disenchantment with the organs of the state, from the Bureau of Employment to the local council to the police force. From an early age I wondered why people accepted these unfair conditions. I felt that things must change or be made to change. Such an opportunity seemed to present itself in the early 1950s.

Living With History

No party was complete in those days without a sing-song, a recitation or two and some music. Songs like 'The Croppy

Boy', 'Kevin Barry' and 'Boolavogue' were great favourites. The volume of singing was often reduced, however, for fear that a passing RUC patrol might raid the house if they heard it. Many houses had a copy of that iconic picture of the Mass Rock with the peasant people surrounding the priest at prayer while on the hill men kept lookout for the Redcoats, the symbol of tyranny. The Penal Laws, the expulsion and execution of priests, the hanging, drawing and quartering of St Oliver Plunkett – these symbols represented the deep and widespread disaffection of Catholics with the Stormont government. After the Second World War there was a reawakening of nationalist fervour, accompanied by much rhetoric. The Anti-Partition League held many meetings, creating headlines in local nationalist newspapers and perhaps also creating great expectations that the problems caused by partition could be resolved. One thing was clear: things would have to change. Youthful energetic opposition to partition led to law-abiding forms of protest. Alongside this was the vocal representation at Stormont which highlighted what had to be done.

However, the lack of any progress was the reason for us cheering the more direct methods of the resurgent republican movement. Most commentators believed that the IRA had been vanquished by the executions, imprisonment and internment of its members during the Second World War. In the South the draconian Offences Against the State Act introduced by de Valera's Fianna Fáil government had practically wiped out the republican movement. In 1946 Seán McCaughey from Tyrone was allowed to die in Portlaoise Prison as a result of a hunger and thirst strike.

Just eight years later, however, the IRA raided the Armagh British Army Barracks and seized a large quantity of armaments. It was a source of great embarrassment to both the Stormont and London governments. I was only fourteen at the time but this raid captured my imagination. It was the first tangible act of militant opposition to British rule in the Six Counties, and the fact that no one had been killed or injured was a source of some satisfaction. Charlie Murphy from Dublin, a member of the IRA Army Council, led the raid with about twenty men, all Dublin based, which was about half the total number of Dublin IRA men. During the raid the IRA took eighteen British soldiers and one civilian captive, locking them up in the emptied armoury.

In the same month in 1954 Liam Kelly from Pomeroy, County Tyrone, was appointed to a seat in the Irish Senate (Seanad Éireann). Liam had been elected to Stormont the previous year but was immediately arrested for alleged sedition in his pre-election speeches and sentenced to twelve months' imprisonment. This enraged people throughout the country, and especially in Tyrone. Having fallen out with the Dublin IRA due to their lack of activity, Liam had formed a splinter republican group in the North. On his release from Crumlin Road Gaol in August 1954 a massive gathering in Pomeroy welcomed him home. The Tricolour was flown, in contravention of the Flags and Emblems Bill, in a town that was almost totally nationalist. This was regarded by the authorities as an act of defiance, and when the RUC waded in with truncheons drawn to capture the flag all hell broke loose.

The confluence of the successful Armagh raid, the riots and prosecutions that followed Liam Kelly's release and his subsequent selection in the South politicised County Tyrone in particular and brought to the fore the natural, latent leanings towards physical force so admired in previous generations. From then on, every year had a new expression of this. In 1955 Brendan O'Boyle was killed when the bomb he was transporting to Stormont in an attempt to blow up the parliament building went off prematurely. Brendan had formed yet another splinter group, Laochra Uladh (Warriors of Ulster). Ulster men were obviously anxious for the fight. This impatience would, in turn, bring forward the planned IRA campaign to December 1956 in which I was involved.

In October 1954, full of confidence after the successful Armagh raid, the IRA planned an attack on Omagh's St Lucia

Barracks, which housed the Royal Inniskilling Fusiliers, many of whom came from the Republic of Ireland. During the course of the raid, however, a British soldier sentry was threatened with a knife to his throat and, whether through fear or bravery, screamed so loudly in the stillness of the night that the camp was awakened. A gun battle ensued as the IRA Volunteers abandoned their plans. In the ensuing uproar the IRA transport departed without at least eight of its members.

The Omagh raid was a chaotic failure that was further compounded by having little or no local support. In the days that followed, eight men from the South were captured and charged with treason felony. Five British soldiers were wounded, most of whom came from the Republic. The trial took place in Omagh Courthouse and crowds gathered on every occasion to cheer the men and jeer the police. During their frequent court appearances the men refused to recognise the right of the British court to try them. An unpleasant aspect was that their private correspondence from Crumlin Road Gaol was passed on to the RUC and read out in court. This was done to embarrass them and revealed again the ability of the authorities to 'spin' events to their advantage. The public was barred from attending the trials and even then there were secret hearings of evidence from which newspaper reporters were barred.

The charging of the men with treason and felony, the formidable show of strength when taking them to court, the secret sessions and the long sentences – twelve years for the leader, Éamonn Boyce, and ten years for the other seven men – galvanised the nationalist people and brought the IRA many recruits in the years ahead. As happened so often in Irish history, the heavy hand of the occupying forces following the Omagh raid made martyrs of the eight prisoners. I remember my father comforting me as I cried on hearing the news on the radio of the sentences handed down to the men who were, in my view, fighting for us. Little did I think that I would be with those men in prison within three years.

5

RESURGENT REPUBLICANISM

Felons Elected in Imperial Westminster Elections

During the 1955 Westminster elections, Sinn Féin came centre
stage in the North, putting up candidates in every
constituency. Tom Mitchell and Philip Clarke, IRA prisoners
in Crumlin Road Gaol, were chosen for Mid-Ulster and
Fermanagh–South Tyrone respectively. It was at this time that
I came into close contact with senior republican leaders mostly
based in Dublin. Although only a teenager, I did more work
for the election of Tom Mitchell than many older than me.
Omagh, being the county town, was the centre for the
publicity campaign and the eventual count. To offset the
chances of any irregularities, it was agreed that as many Sinn
Féiners as possible should be present at the count. To secure
representation at the count, however, it was compulsory to
have the signature of a Justice of the Peace confirming the
identity of the person. This task was undertaken by me. With
a bundle of blank forms I cycled out to a retired RIC/RUC
sergeant called Flanagan. The Flanagans and Donnellys would
have been on friendly terms. I promised Sergeant Flanagan
faithfully that only those whom I deemed suitable would be
given one of the signed forms to complete. Warning me not
to let the forms out of my possession, he duly signed the lot.

I often think back with embarrassment at my putting such a decent man in that position. In 1979 Sergeant Flanagan's son Peter, who had also joined the RUC, was murdered by a self-confessed IRA informer. When I heard the shocking news, I thought of the goodwill his father had shown years before towards republicans in prison and how it now counted for nothing.

As a member of the junior branch of the Legion of Mary I sold the Catholic newspapers every Sunday around town and as a consequence I became very familiar with the houses of Omagh and those who lived there. The most useful election task for me was to accompany one of the southern canvassers. I knew where we would be welcome and where we would not. The canvassers insisted on calling on every house and on one occasion I was with Sinn Féin Vice-President Tom Doyle from Dublin when we called to the house of Vincent Murnaghan, an architect of great distinction. But as soon as Tom started to speak, Mr Murnaghan simply turned on his heel and walked back into the house. This was my first experience of meeting someone from our own community whose views obviously did not coincide with mine. Tom asked me if Mr Murnaghan had a brother a judge in Dublin. When I confirmed that he had, he began to laugh, and confided that Judge Murnaghan had sentenced him to ten years in prison for his part in the Phoenix Park armoury raid in 1939.

The results of the election were overwhelming for all of us. Both Tom Mitchell and Philip Clarke were elected, albeit by slim majorities, with Mitchell defeating the Unionist Charles Beatty. Most historical comment centres on the Bobby Sands victory in 1981 as the first time a serving prisoner was elected to Westminster, but in fact it happened over twenty years earlier in two constituencies. Worth noting is the fact that Sinn Féin managed a total of 152,000 votes as they put up candidates in all the constituencies, even those where they had no chance of victory. This demonstrated a great dissatisfaction with the Unionist-controlled Stormont government to the point where ordinary peace-loving people were prepared to cast their vote for candidates most of whom were imprisoned for using force against the state. But this vital message was lost on both the British and Stormont governments. If they had analysed this phenomenon properly and taken steps to eliminate the obvious injustices, they may have prevented both the 1956 campaign and the eventual thirty years of 'Troubles'.

Shocked by the outcome of the elections in the North, the authorities in London dusted down an old statute that outlawed any 'convicted felon' from being a member of the Westminster parliament. So Tom Mitchell was unceremoniously unseated by a British court (as was Philip Clarke) despite the fact that almost 30,000 people in Mid-Ulster had voted for him. A new by-election date of 11 August 1955 was arranged for the Mid-Ulster constituency. In the by-election campaign I redoubled my efforts and met many of the Sinn Féin activists from the South who came to canvass. We knew that we would succeed again since the British had by now angered most nationalists. At that time of the year many Tyrone people were on holidays in Bundoran, County Donegal, so one of my tasks was to go to Bundoran and coordinate transport by car for as many people as were willing to return to Tyrone to vote. Cars were scarce at that time and private bus companies virtually unknown. But the railway line between Omagh and Bundoran was still in operation and was a great boon to my efforts. We needed to be able to get people back to Tyrone on polling day and return them to Bundoran the same day to continue their holiday. Master O'Brien and 'Shaw' Carty were my guides and we visited every guesthouse, caravan and hotel in Bundoran and encouraged those entitled to vote to come back on election day. They did so in their droves. It was an exhilarating experience in planning that undoubtedly helped my formation. The result was an even bigger victory for Tom Mitchell, celebrated by nationalists throughout the county. In Omagh we had a bonfire in the middle of St Patrick's Street, the first 'nationalist' bonfire I remember since the Tyrone minors won the All Ireland in 1948.

At this time the B Specials were very active, stopping cars and asking people to identify themselves, while knowing full well who they were. In March 1955 nineteen-year-old Arthur Leonard was shot dead while driving home with three others. The B Specials had set up a roadblock in Armagh, and as Arthur came to a halt an RUC marksman shot him dead and wounded one of his passengers, Clare Mallon. No one was ever charged. The whole country was horrified, and no one was prepared to believe that it was not deliberate. The incident led to widespread dismay and anger among nationalists and, coupled with the political events described above, an ever-increasing feeling that we were living in a 'them' and 'us' society.

Tomás Mac Giolla of Sinn Féin summed it up for many when he gave a speech on the steps of Omagh Courthouse in 1956: 'If you are a farmer and you have four fields and a bigger farmer comes and takes over one of your fields, do you go cap in hand and ask him politely to leave your field – or do you get your shotgun and tell him to get off your property or you will blow his head off?'

In May 1956 there was another by-election in Mid-Ulster to replace the Unionist Charles Beatty. A farmer and auctioneer, Beatty was deemed to be holding 'an office of profit under the Crown' and was forced to resign his seat. The Unionists managed to defeat the Sinn Féin candidate, owing to a split Nationalist vote, and held the seat, and the British government was relieved that another coup of Irish republicanism had been avoided. Stormont and Westminster thought they had now finished the 'Mitchell Affair' by having him unseated by a Unionist. But their real trouble was only beginning. The authorities had not shown the slightest understanding of the situation. The nationalist people in the North were getting off their knees. Within seven months of that election a campaign of physical resistance would be in full swing against the British regime in Ireland.

Rising Expectations

From 1954 the IRA Army Council had held training camps to prepare Volunteers for the coming fight. Electoral success in Tyrone and Fermanagh brought more Volunteers from every one of the thirty-two counties and training camps were becoming more sophisticated with the arrival from America of Seán Cronin, a journalist and former officer in the Irish Army who had returned to join the IRA at the highest level. In the summer of 1956 the Army Council decided to activate a campaign in the Six Counties.

A series of events challenging British rule in Ireland indicated the level of unrest. These included stunts like the taking of Hugh Lane pictures from the National Gallery in London by a republican splinter group headed by Joe Christle. More serious incidents included an IRA raid on the Arbourfield Army Barracks in England in August 1955 and an unsuccessful attack on Rosslea RUC Barracks in November 1955 by another splinter group, Saor Uladh, under the leadership of Liam Kelly. Kelly and Christle were continuously raising the bar and putting it up to the IRA, and there is no doubt that the IRA Army Council made a hasty decision in launching Operation Harvest before all was ready.

IRA Chief of Staff Tony Magan was totally intolerant of Christle. This led to serious animosity between the two groups with many of the Dublin IRA defecting to Christle's organisation. On 11 November 1956, in what may have been the catalyst for the Army Council to launch their campaign, Saor Uladh and Christle's faction combined to carry out attacks on six customs posts along the border.

Following the surge in recruitment following the election campaigns, the IRA sent many Volunteers into the Six Counties and initiated training programmes – how to handle a Lee Enfield rifle and Thompson sub-machine gun, how to walk in the dark, scramble up and down hills and walk on one's hunkers with weapon in hand. There were the usual fitness techniques and some fairly explicit hand-to-hand fighting skills. One of our trainers was a tall, nineteen-year-old Corkman of high intellect named Dave O'Connell, more popularly known in later years as Daithí Ó Conaill. Our paths crossed again for a short time when he arrived rather late in the campaign into A Wing in Crumlin Road having been sentenced to eight years when captured in an RUC ambush in County Tyrone in 1959 in which he was seriously wounded.

We were taught how to make bombs using gelignite, detonators and fuse wire. The plan of campaign obviously saw the need for gelignite to blow up bridges, telephone exchanges and other communication links in order to isolate the police and army. I became rather adept at this skill but in that campaign no one was injured or killed by a bomb except some Volunteers whose bombs exploded prematurely.

Operation Harvest stipulated that four mobile columns of full-time trained Volunteers of twenty-five men per column would lead each attack, hitting selected targets, aided by units of local men acting in support. The methodology was guerilla warfare – hit and hide, hit and hide again and move on. The purpose was to destroy all communications links, enemy vehicles, supply sources including petrol stations and strategic administration buildings. In addition, leaflets would be distributed to encourage the civilian population to show resistance and by so doing liberate large areas of the Six Counties.

Apart from the obvious sense of urgency at home, the fact that revolution was in the air in many parts of the world was also an important factor and one that is often overlooked by historians. Castro was fighting a war for the common people and strove to overthrow the dictator Batista in Cuba. Algerians had formed the FLN and were fighting a horrible war with France to achieve independence. EOKA (an organisation much like the IRA) was fighting against the occupation of Cyprus by the British and seeking union with Greece. African countries were calling for an end to colonisation. Hungarians had risen in rebellion, in October 1956, against their

Communist government and Soviet control over their lives. In 1956 the British had invaded Egypt but eventually had to withdraw, leaving their arch-enemy Gamal Nasser still in charge. As a young fellow I admired Castro and Nasser and read every report avidly.

At home the die was cast and on the night of 12 December 1956 a physical force campaign to free the Six Counties from British rule was launched. I was told to find my way to a place between Glenhordial and Greencastle and to wear warm clothes and good boots. I told my mother that I was going to see some pals outside the town and would be back late.

Operation Harvest Begins

The headquarters for the launch was an old deserted building in the hills above Omagh. As well as locals, the party of twenty or so men came from Dublin, Cork, Wexford and Limerick, most of whom were strangers to me. I assumed that Gerry Higginbothem from Dublin was in charge and when I asked him what was afoot, he explained that Patrick (Paddy) Webster, also from Dublin, was joint Officer Commanding (O/C). I had never met Webster and afterwards I learned that he had been in the British Army and had served in Omagh Barracks.

The locals were Charlie Ferris, John McMahon, Charlie Harlay, John Woods, myself and some others from Mountfield. The flying column consisted of Gerry Higginbothem, Paddy Webster, Timmy Conlan, John Henderson from Dublin and Brendan O'Neill, Jim Lane, Charlie Ronayne, Noel Roche, Jackie McManus of Cork, Willie Gleeson from Limerick, and Ted Morrissey of Wexford.

At some stage several of the group left to collect a lorry and it was understood that on their return we would attack the St Lucia Barracks in Omagh. I could not believe it, as even then I thought that a rehearsal plan should have preceded such a daring action. The barracks had been attacked just two years earlier and no doubt fortifications would have been strengthened and early warning systems employed. Granted that secrecy was of paramount importance, a discussion with us locals about the best plan of action would no doubt have been beneficial. Nevertheless, it was now a case of obeying orders as we were divided into different groups – those guarding the area, those who went in search of transport and those who would be the vanguard of the attack.

As we lay in the ditches some concern was raised about the length of time it was taking the lads to obtain the lorry. Then, all of a sudden, the earth shook and in the distance we could hear a bomb going off and after a short time another muffled noise like distant thunder. Operation Harvest had commenced. Not long afterwards we were assembled and told that the unit had failed to acquire the targeted lorry and that the element of surprise was now lost. In these circumstances the best action was for the locals to disperse to their homes and for the flying column to seek a safe base further up in the Sperrin Mountains. There was no Plan B. For example, in the event that the barracks could not be attacked some other more accessible targets could have been destroyed. It showed a lack of micro-planning on the part of the Army Council. The column successfully retreated and covered some distance without losing a single gun or man. The RUC and B Specials combed the mountains in the following days and the column had a real challenge to avoid being caught, all the while enduring bitterly cold conditions.

The next day the papers were full of the events of the night before. Magherafelt Courthouse had been blown up in County Derry, a B Special hall had been burned down in Newry, a British Army territorial building bombed in Enniskillen and two bridges partially blown up in other parts of County Fermanagh. The most adventurous target of the night was the RAF radar installation at Torr Head in the Glens of Antrim. Three Corkmen were captured in the attempted attack. A BBC station in Derry city was destroyed by a five-man unit who were only advised of the campaign some hours before. In Armagh a similar plan to ours in Omagh had been agreed for the barracks there. However, the column had the same difficulty in securing a lorry and eventually only acquired one of dubious vintage and reliability that was unfit for an attack. This proved a blessing in disguise, however, as security at the barracks had been greatly improved following a raid two years previously, and if the column had launched an attack they would undoubtedly have walked into a bloody ambush. There were other incidents that night also, and the overall effect was significant. The scale and spread of the attacks and the manpower committed left the authorities in no doubt that the fight for Irish freedom was on again.

As most people did not have television in those days, newspapers were relied on for information. Editorials in papers North and South boomed that such a physical force campaign was immoral, unjustified and doomed to failure. Those of us anxious to change the rotten structure of the North, however, were exhilarated by events. The following night the Fermanagh IRA attacked two RUC police stations in Lisnaskea and Derrylin and blew up several more bridges as part of the plan to isolate the enemy. Stormont outlawed Sinn Féin, which only strengthened the resolve of republicans and encouraged people to join the IRA. I was secretary of the local Sinn Féin cumann (club), set up during the election campaigns for Tom Mitchell, and we had an office in John Street, Omagh, five doors down from the RUC station. The day the government made it a crime to belong to Sinn Féin, myself and Charlie McMenamin went to the office and burned all documentation in the fireplace. We also brought the Tricolour to a safe place, as it was banned under the Northern Ireland Flags and Emblems Bill.

The banning of Sinn Féin coincided with the decision of the Stormont government to reintroduce interment without trial, and over the following days the RUC began rounding up people, mostly from their homes in the early hours of the morning. Anyone associated with the Irish language, Irish

dancing or any other aspect of Irish culture was at their mercy.
Although some active Volunteers were brought in, RUC
intelligence was generally poor, resulting in very many people
being incarcerated who had no connection with the IRA
whatsoever.

The activity of the IRA in Fermanagh was a daily
reminder to the authorities that the campaign was here to stay.
A proclamation issued on the day the campaign started declared
that the IRA would 'fight until the invader is driven from our
soil and victory ours'. In mid-December Prime Minister
Anthony Eden reiterated in the House of Commons that the
Six Counties was an integral part of the United Kingdom.

Reality of Death

In late 1956 the British government implored Taoiseach John
A. Costello and his government to help stamp out the IRA.
Although the Gardaí were already very active, the general
feeling in the Republic remained supportive of the struggle to
free the Six Counties. The IRA's public pledge not to resist or
harm any Garda stood them in good stead, while Volunteers
were also instructed not to injure or kill RUC or B Specials if
at all avoidable. On 30 December, however, RUC Constable
John Scally was shot dead when a gun battle ensued during an
IRA raid on Derrylin RUC station. Condemnation came
from Church, state and media, and I remember being
disturbed by the killing of 'one of our own' and going into
the Sacred Heart Church to pray for him and his family while
still going on to organise locally for the IRA. A second RUC
officer was killed in July 1957, and two days later internment
was introduced in the South by de Valera's Fianna Fáil
government.

We had no leader in west Tyrone at that time and some of
us rather cautiously met to establish if the flying column was
coming back and what was expected of us now. On one
occasion in early January I cycled to a Volunteer's house near
Mountfield, and as his mother made us tea in the kitchen he

told me that he and another Volunteer had burned down Mountfield Lodge in the early hours of the morning. A mansion belonging to Major General D. G. Moore of the British Army, Mountfield Lodge was rumoured to station British troops. While I was in the house, the RUC and B Specials burst in, questioned me and arrested the young man. When the police departed I cycled to Mountfield on the pretence of carrying out an errand for the woman of the house and through a named contact arranged for word to be spread. The burning of Mountfield Lodge went down well locally as no one had been injured and there was now no credible base for enemy forces.

Then came the shocking news of the deaths of Seán South and Feargal O'Hanlon on 31 December 1956 after a failed IRA attack on Brookeborough RUC station. Constable Scally's death was overshadowed and its adverse effects mostly neutralised by the martyrdom of the two Volunteers. Urban and county councils throughout the twenty-six counties passed resolutions of sympathy and some contained words of support for the cause. The funerals of both men were deemed the biggest since those of the fallen in the War of Independence; over 50,000 attended that of 26-year-old Seán South in Limerick, while thousands more gathered to pay respects to Feargal O'Hanlon in Monaghan. The sense of martyrdom was heightened by unverified stories of B Special and RUC Special Branch men mutilating the dead bodies, which made us even more determined to win the war and avenge their deaths.

Given the rising sympathy and admiration for the resistance campaign among the people in the South, Costello's interparty government issued a statement that there was only one army in the state and that they were not at war with Britain. The campaign continued through January 1957 with a morale-boosting operation in Dungannon where the relatively new British Army barracks was blown up. However, the IRA's activities were seriously hampered by the actions of the Republic's Gardaí and military in border areas.

6

FIRST TASTE OF PRISON

In February 1957 the republican movement issued another message to the people of Ireland, the distribution of which had unfortunate consequences for me and some friends. The statement was printed on handbills which were to be stuck on telegraph posts and shop windows and pushed through letterboxes throughout the Six Counties. When I received the bills I arranged to have them put all around the town of Omagh and enlisted the help of three friends, two of whom had no connection with Sinn Féin or the IRA.

The printed statement was the well-known call for independence and an invitation to Protestants to join in a new Ireland. But as we distributed near Omagh's Market Street, two RUC men arrested us and brought us to the station. We were detained there overnight in stinking cells and the next day brought to Crumlin Road Gaol in Belfast in a typical over-the-top reaction on the part of the authorities. On arrival we were treated like common criminals, even though we were as yet not charged with any offence. I was issued with a detention order, as was one of the others, Seán Woods, and we were both sent to C Wing. Detention orders allowed the authorities to hold prisoners indefinitely until it was decided to charge, intern without trial or release them. Most prisoners were detained for months in very strict, remand-type conditions. After several weeks I was charged with incitement and placed on remand.

If detention was bad, being on remand was worse. We were frogmarched everywhere by unsympathetic warders who shouted 'No talking'. We were locked up for almost two months during which we were confined to our cells for twenty hours a day. We were allowed out to walk, in single file ten paces behind the person in front, for about two hours in the morning and one and a half hours in the evening. There was no dining room, so we ate alone in our cells. Breakfast consisted of porridge with a quarter mug of milk, a mug of tea and a piece of bread. Dinner was soup followed by meat, vegetables and potatoes. Dessert was custard, prunes or semolina, made solely from water. All were served in 'dixies' or round aluminium containers. Tea was a lump of bread and a mug of tea and sometimes a piece of cheese. I took refuge in reading and, as I was still at school preparing to sit my Senior Examination in June, I studied a little better than I did at home. While on remand I met John Kelly, with whom I would later plan the escape. John, along with three others, had been arrested in December 1956 in possession of arms in Tyrone some weeks previously.

John Woods, a cousin of Seán Woods, was one of the four arrested for putting up posters but he was charged by the RUC for having bullets in his house. He was sentenced to imprisonment and later interned. The rest of us were brought to a Belfast court where a solicitor from Omagh, without any consultation with me, made the case that we were only teenagers and the magistrate released us with a warning not to be gulled by shibboleths. If I could only understand him! The next day at school I looked up the word. It means a catchword which is usually an old-fashioned doctrine or formula of a party or sect. My action in allowing the solicitor to speak up for me was a recognition of a British court, something which would come back to haunt me later. My father and mother were with me on the train home, where I received a great welcome from friends, neighbours and people I met for the first time.

Back to the Fight: B Specials and their Drill Halls

Almost immediately I was in touch with my fellow Volunteers and keen to resume the fight for freedom. Contrary to common expectations, I was never asked to participate in any formal joining-up ceremony or given a copy of the Green Book, the IRA handbook that provided training suggestions and counter-interrogation techniques. This reflects the lack of organisation and preparedness for the campaign in 1956.

As there was now no flying column of southern men anywhere in west Tyrone we decided to recruit locally and develop our own unit. In May and June 1957 a training camp was arranged in Monaghan. I had been trained previously on the methodology of bomb making and could now pass this knowledge on to others. We had decided that the most effective use of our manpower and resources was to select targets that would meet with the approval of the nationalist community and to avoid injury and death. Targets such as tax offices and B Special drill halls were identified.

In the pantheon of hate figures for nationalists, none was regarded with more contempt than the B men. When established, the RUC had three kinds of special constables: A, B and C. The A constables were full-time and paid; the B Specials were unpaid, armed part-timers whose duties included one night of service, usually roadblocks, drill once a week and occasional emergency day duties; C Specials were armed and were available for emergencies only. B and C Specials received generous clothing allowances and other perks. The A and C Specials did not survive long but the B men went from strength to strength until 1970.

The B Specials, boycotted by Catholics, were regarded by most unionists as their bulwark against republican revolutionaries. In 1957 there were 10,000 B men in service. Their modus operandi was to erect a roadblock, usually in a nationalist area, and stop all cyclists and motorists. They assumed the power to question and detain, and were always armed with Webley revolvers, Lee Enfield rifles and later with

Sten guns. They approached the vehicle or person in groups of two or three while the others remained in the shadows with guns at the ready. Even when they knew the name of the person, they insisted on full questioning and often indulged in insults about the person or family members. Complaints were useless; B men were a law unto themselves with seemingly no accountability to any higher power. Their arrogance and visual display of domination was a constant 'dagger in the soul' of Catholics. Individually, as neighbours one could not find better people, but when they donned the uniform they became a malign presence.

The murder of Arthur Leonard in 1955 was a reminder to us all that the B men could kill the innocent and get away with it. Their existence was a manifestation of the 'siege mentality'. Their ancestors had come to Ireland some 300 years earlier with the various plantations of Ulster and took the fertile land from the native Irish. In 1632, 70 per cent of land in Ireland was owned by Catholics but by 1745 that had been reduced to 5 per cent. It was a 'land grab' of extraordinary proportions. They had pushed the natives into the hills, from which they would come down on a dark night and plunder the Planters' farms, steal cattle or burn a barn. The Planters were afraid and, centuries later, their inheritors were still afraid, but did not know why. They always needed to have guns around the house to protect them. They needed to establish who was in their neighbourhood and what was their business.

In 1970 as part of the Civil Rights campaign the dissolution of the B Specials was achieved. Their successor, the Ulster Defence Regiment (UDR), was eventually also disbanded when it was clearly established that these were the same personnel as the B men who could not change their ways or accept accountability.

In 1957 we planned our own campaign against the B Specials. It was summer and nothing had been heard from the flying squad or General Headquarters (GHQ) in Dublin for many months. We did know that Gerry Higginbothem, our best bet for continuing operations, had been arrested near Strabane. Consequently, IRA chiefs in Dublin had been effectively cut off from us and in those days travel was neither easily accessible nor cheap. So we made our own plans. Despite my youth I had developed an unshakable confidence in my ability to make decisions. Once I had analysed a situation and considered the strengths and weaknesses of it, I entertained no doubts.

It was decided that a local group would have neither the training nor equipment to carry out an attack on the army, and that our best course of action was to identify and destroy B Special drill halls in west Tyrone. The objective was to deprive the B men of a regular shelter, make it difficult for them to train and to frighten them off the roads. By so doing we would be clearly performing one of Operation Harvest's main aims – to clear districts of British forces and their allies. This clearance would provide flying columns with reasonably safe passage back to the centre of the North. In addition, successful operations against the B Specials would help attract supporters among the general public back to the campaign, which had lost much of its lustre since January 1957.

It was our intention to blow up every B Special drill hall in County Tyrone. That aim, however, presented a few problems. The Specials did not have drill halls everywhere and so in some parts used Orange Lodges and Church of Ireland halls for their activity. We had no wish to make it easy for the Stormont government to misrepresent us as sectarian. Our fight was not with their religion but with the domination of our people by Britain which denied us a united Ireland. We also had to implement the IRA's order to avoid any bloodshed of Irish men or women. That placed another burden on us as we had to ensure that the halls would be destroyed when empty, and that was usually late at night. This gave us challenging logistical issues to consider as it was always our aim that Volunteers should be safe from attack or arrest in the carrying out of operations. The destruction of the drill halls began in earnest in July 1957.

Fermanagh IRA were advised of our plans and they organised similar activity. Logistically it was agreed to keep the initial plans simple – select a target, prepare an entry plan and an exit strategy, agree the team and set the date. The chosen material for bomb making was gelignite, an inert substance that was only dangerous when a fuse and detonator were inserted into the material mass. However, when engaged it constituted a serious risk when transporting or carrying it. During the 1956–62 campaign, also called the 'Border Campaign', six republicans were killed by bombs in their possession. In at least one case the Volunteer tied the gelignite bomb, with fuse and detonator inserted, around his neck while he climbed over ditches to gain access to the target. The wonder is that there were not more people killed accidentally during those years.

Contact was made with the groups in different localities to establish how the various targets could be best hit. Travel had to be done at night, which presented difficulties given the B Specials' random roadblocks. My job was to make up the bomb and leave it at a convenient place for collection. The team would then transport the bomb to the designated hall and place it in the best position to ensure complete destruction. The men who carried out these operations usually lived not far from the target and before placing the device would reconnoitre the hall to ensure that no one was in it or in the vicinity. The halls targeted were in Beragh, Eskra, Fintona and Skelga. The newspapers were full of these activities as they showed the IRA's ability to strike night after night and week after week. Alongside these reports were details of explosions in drill halls in east Tyrone and Fermanagh.

Thrilled at our success, we planned a more dramatic attack and decided on Omagh's RUC station. Using other groups who were not directly connected to us, a plan was prepared. However, the requirement not to cause injury to RUC or civilians caused this particular operation ultimately to be cancelled at a late stage. An important aspect of our structure was that it presaged the cell-like system developed by other revolutionary armies and indeed later by the Provisional IRA. While it did not operate strictly like a cell, in many instances other activists involved were unknown to us.

Lack of secrecy would eventually break up our local organisation. Most of us were very young, indeed teenagers, and there was not a clear understanding that secrecy was paramount. Either in the interests of gaining more Volunteers or just simply boasting, the plain fact is that people who had no involvement with us heard about our activities. I was warned about this and told a section of the group that if the loose talk was not stopped we would all end up in Crumlin Road Gaol, words that were referred to later in evidence in the courthouse in Belfast. My warning, however, was too late. Special Branch had enough hearsay to arrest a number of people, and the lack of training for Volunteers in counteracting RUC interrogation techniques was a serious omission.

In the weeks that followed, a flying column member, Pat Haughian from Lurgan, arrived in west Tyrone and I received word that he wanted to see me. We discussed our activity and escalation plans and when I was leaving he gave me a parcel of handbills with the latest message from the IRA for distribution. Remembering my previous experience, I took them rather reluctantly and at home placed them safely in the bin at our back door. I thought that if the house was raided I could say that I binned them on receipt, although I wrapped them carefully as my intention was to distribute them.

The following morning at six o'clock we were woken by loud knocking at the door. Looking out I saw policemen all around the house. They arrested me and searched the house, including the bins, but did not find the bills. I was taken to Omagh police station and held in the filthy, windowless cells in the basement. The blanket they gave me was thick with dirt and the only light was a low-watt bulb high up in the ceiling, protected by a grille. The bed was a piece of wood that seemed to be nailed to the floor and wall. I was kept there until night time and was only given food that my mother had left in. I was taken from my cell and questioned by Head Constable Detective McCappin in the company of about six other policemen. They revealed some of what they knew and looked for confirmation from me, but all I confirmed was my name and address. Some detectives began shouting at me while others pestered me with questions. Then suddenly all but one constable left. On a table nearby was a revolver. I did consider making a grab for it and attempting an escape, but realised that it was most likely unloaded and left there with that very intention in mind. I'll never know. After some time I was brought back to the cells below ground.

In the middle of the night about six policemen brought me out, threw me in a car and took me to Beragh police station, where once again I was thrown into a cell. This was part of the deliberate disorientating technique of RUC interrogation. After an hour I was dragged out of the cell to a room filled with policemen, led once again by McCappin. They continued the same line of questioning, revealing a little more of what they knew – again looking for confirmation. They also, of course, added material that was not true in relation to earlier operations outside the county. This is the kind of interrogation that led to the infamous miscarriages of justice in England in later years. Getting nowhere, however, they brought me back to the cell but shortly afterwards pushed me out again and into a Black Maria, a vehicle designed in such a way that prisoners can neither be seen from outside nor see out, except through a small window up high. My new destination was Ballygawley police station. It was the same routine once again, and at this stage I was losing track of time and place.

Some time later I was aroused again and brought to Clogher police station. Bringing me from town to town prevented any nationalist solicitor, or indeed any member of my family seeking me out to support me. At the age of seventeen, I should have been offered the opportunity to contact a solicitor or family member. In Clogher the whole assembly of interrogators was there in force, and they told me they had proof I was in the IRA. Eventually I was left with just one uniformed sergeant. I told him that I would only admit to at one time being in the IRA but that I had since left it. I was subsequently charged, not only with IRA membership but also conspiracy to cause explosions, as were nine others rounded up at the same time.

It was the end of the road for Operation Harvest in west Tyrone and we were most disappointed at having had such a short span of activity. We had not, collectively or individually, taken enough precautions and in this I may have been complacent myself. We also lacked in-depth counter-interrogation training that should be mandatory for all revolutionaries.

On arrival at Crumlin Road, being processed through the system was a most humiliating and degrading experience. I was given a number – 1082 – that would be my identification while in prison. It is a number that will remain imprinted on my brain until the day I die. I was brought down to Reception where a prison officer took some personal details. Some belongings were placed in a box and I was told that these would be given back to me on my release. They never were. Then I was marched down with others to the cell reception area. I was told to strip and they looked for birthmarks and operation marks so that I could be identified in case of escape or some worse fate. The area had a number of baths which were sheltered only slightly but still visible to the warders and orderlies. After a bath we were given our clothes back before each prisoner was assigned a cell.

At this time the prison was being filled with political prisoners. It was bonanza time for petty criminals who were serving two years or less as they were released before their normal release date to make way for the likes of us. Prisoners detained or on remand were housed two to a cell. I shared with Seán McHugh from Beragh, who was eventually sentenced to eight years. He was good company and made up for the lack of exercise or other association. But then a ruling came across to us from D Wing that we were to demand separate cells in order to put the prison authorities under space pressure. It must have been a prisoner's right then as our demand was acceded to immediately. We were now truly isolated until after our first court hearing.

The first visit to Crumlin Road Courthouse was via the notorious tunnel. Dimly lit and damp, it was nevertheless an amazing structure and a triumph, no doubt, for the architect responsible. It was made of red bricks and the curved walls were perfect. It was underground and ran from the prison right into the courthouse cells below the dock where prisoners are taken for trial. We had a sense of foreboding as we walked along that neither justice nor mercy were in the minds of those who created this tunnel. And the misery of the tunnel would be well matched by the sternness of judgement delivered by our enemies. When we surfaced in the courthouse on this first occasion we were brought to Court number 2 which resembled a room in a Georgian building with its high ceiling and sense of space. The Special Powers Act allowed the authorities to change the venue of the court so as to ensure a conviction. If the case had been tried in Omagh, no true Tyrone jury would have convicted us. All ten of us were bound together by the common charge of conspiracy to cause explosions. This was a British stratagem to tie everybody in with this 'catch all' charge so that any evidence against one would be valid against another when it came to sentencing.

7

PRISON LIFE

Queen Versus Daniel Donnelly: Belfast City Commissions

Resident Magistrate (RM) G. C. Lynn was very hostile to us despite the fact that his job was to be even handed. This hostility manifested itself in his cavalier attitude to anyone who attempted to speak out against blatant untruths. Because one witness, who was a minor, did not confirm what the RUC wanted to prove, the RM immediately declared him a hostile witness. He actually bullied the boy and when solicitor Harry McDevitt, who was not representing the boy, rose and objected strongly, it was the only time he was silenced. I could have clapped McDevitt on the back. He was not afraid of them and there were not too many solicitors like him. When some of the RUC men were giving evidence from a written script the RM read his newspaper. We were arraigned before the court on two rows of chairs with our backs to the wall, surrounded by RUC and prison officers. There was great media interest in the case and the journalists were packed into two rows of chairs at right angles to us. At the end of each day we were marched back through the tunnel to C Wing, where we were lucky to receive some cold food.

On the third day I spotted an opportunity to escape which

I regretted not attempting. When the court finished and as the RM left the room there were usually animated conversations among ourselves as it was our only opportunity to talk together since we were on remand. The journalists and those guarding us relaxed and chatted loudly also. As the journalists walked to the door I noticed that they were not being individually scrutinised by the police as they left. I was at the end of our row and as the last journalists were leaving I had the opportunity to duck under the table and walk out as if I was one of them. The police and warders were engaged in conversation and I have no doubt that the other journalists would have looked the other way. But I hesitated, and the opportunity evaporated.

The charge against me read as follows:

The Queen versus Daniel Ignatius Donnelly

Court of Belfast City Commission. Date: 15th of October 1957

Statement of Offence: Being and remaining a member of an unlawful association contrary to regulation 24A of the Regulations made under the Civil Authorities (Special Powers) Acts (Northern Ireland) 1932–43. [The date reference was obliterated, and written in hand was '1922–43 note amended by order of the Courts'.]

Particular of Offence: Daniel Ignatius Donnelly, between the months of May and August 1957 was and remained a member of an organisation, to wit, the Irish Republican Army, deemed to be an unlawful association.

Witnesses: Sergeant Kerr Patterson, Constable Patrick Sheppard, Sergeant Stanley J. Kernaghan.

The second charge against me, and indeed against all the others, which was dropped in January 1958, was as follows:

Conspiracy to cause explosions contrary to Section 3(a) of the Explosive Substance Act 1883. That on diverse dates between the 1st day of May 1957 and the 31st of July 1957 conspired together and with other persons unknown to cause by gelignite or other explosive substance an explosion in the United Kingdom of a nature likely to endanger life or to cause serious injury to property.

The authorities' devious use of this charge was to ensure that the judge was able to take all of the evidence both proved and unproved when sentencing, even though they had no intention of proceeding with it. Conspiracy charges are universally very difficult to prove and very seldom hold up when challenged, unless there is overwhelming evidence.

Our time before Lord Chief Justice MacDermott began in the main court in Crumlin Road Courthouse. Police and forensic witnesses climbed into the witness boxes as our various cases were heard. The team was headed by the Right Honorable W. Brian Maginess, QC, LLD, MP, Her Majesty's Attorney General. The leading RUC man was District Inspector John Bradley, Clogher, assisted by Sergeant Thomas McCrum, Dungannon, Constable Barrett, Sergeant Kerr Patterson, William Elliot, Constable Harry Woodside and Nathaniel Holmes of the Department of Finance. Holmes' task was to emphasise the enormity of the financial damage done to Eskra B Special drill hall as it had been newly built at a cost of £1,200.

My case was short and bitter. The single charge against me was that I was 'a member of an illegal organisation, the Irish Republican Army'. The conspiracy charge had been deferred and was eventually dropped in January 1958. The RUC witness was Detective Sheppard whom I understood to be a Catholic. I took the stance of declaring: 'I refuse to recognise the jurisdiction of this Court', which effectively gave the jury an easy case to try. The Lord Chief Justice looked at me disdainfully, regarding my stance as an insult to him. I asked Sheppard to confirm my arrest times and the time of my exit from police custody into prison, as I knew that I had been detained beyond the legally allowable limit. He denied my accusation.

The jury took five minutes to find me guilty. Well-dressed men of middle-class stock, they looked at me condescendingly as I stood alone in the dock aged eighteen years (my birthday had been the previous month). When all the cases were dealt with the judge set a day aside for sentencing and so on 22 October 1957 we faced the judge in his Lord Chief Justice crimson robes. I have to say that I thought the sentences would have been two or three years for most of us. If I had been paying attention to the judge's remarks at the official opening of the Belfast City Commissions, however, I may have been better prepared. He talked of the need for harsher sentences for republicans and outlined some of the measures available to the judiciary and pledged his intention to invoke them if necessary.

I was the last to be sentenced. As my comrades came down from the dock with sentences of four, five, six and eight years, the penny was beginning to drop. The Lord Chief Justice asked me if I had anything to say, to which I shook my head. Lord Chief Justice John Clarke MacDermott gazed at me balefully and with the full pomposity of his elevated seat read from a carefully prepared script which would purport to give some rationale for the sentence he intended to give me. He intoned his denunciation of the lawlessness of our activities, he spoke of me as 'the moving spirit' in this whole conspiracy and talked of the need for him and his ilk to defend themselves by reintroducing flogging and even proposed invoking the death penalty. He made much of my grammar school education which he believed made me the leader. 'Your attitude to this court has not been one that suggests that you have turned your back on this sort of business,' he declared. 'There is no doubt that you are a person of some education and it is a thousand pities to see a young fellow like you inducing others to break the law when you would have been better preparing yourself to help your country in some constructive way. It is quite clear to me that you are one of the ring leaders. Parliament has made provision that the manner in which accused like you may be punished includes not only long terms of imprisonment and whipping but the sentence of death.' I listened with growing incredulity as he sentenced me to ten years' imprisonment.

Back through the tunnel we went for the penultimate time, this time to the Reception area again. Until then we had worn our own clothes but now we had to give them up. Convicts lose any rights they enjoyed outside prison and that includes the right to wear your own clothes. We were subjected to the usual demeaning process of bathing and strip-searching before donning our prison garb of underpants, vest, woollen socks, boots, canvas slippers, grey serge tunic consisting of trousers, waistcoat and jacket and a heavy linen striped shirt. We were also given an additional set of underwear, shirt and trousers. All prisoners wore their clothes for a full week before they could be sent to the laundry. My number, 1082, was indelibly stamped on each garment so that they could be identified as mine. We were then brought into the dreaded A Wing and assigned our cells.

High Security A Wing

My first cell was temporary and was on A1 (ground floor) on the football yard side, which meant that B Wing was partially visible and audible. This floor was dull, gloomy and very noisy. One of the immediate impressions of prison is the almost continuous noise of shouting, keys jangling and doors banging. The cell was bare and with a very poor light. We were told that the Governor would see us the following day.

That night of my sentence was the longest. I was working out all the computations, trying to establish when I would be released; 1967 seemed a lifetime away. But with 25 per cent remission for good conduct that would make it 1965 and with a third off it would be 1964. Whatever way I looked at it, for an eighteen-year-old it seemed a terribly long time to be locked up. Without anything to read, I had plenty of time to reflect. With the dull thud of the door closing that day, it is difficult to describe the sense of loneliness I felt. My future teenage years were finished. There were so many things to do and now I would be locked away from my family, my school friends and my comrades outside. The bleakness of my situation came at me in waves and the only thing that prevented tears was the fact that a warder could be looking through the spy hole in the door and I did not want to give him that satisfaction. As things became quiet I turned my mind to my mother and father. Not only did they love me dearly but they held me in high esteem and had great expectations for me. Having been brought up, like most Catholics at the time, with a reverence and belief in prayer, the only consolation was to say the Rosary. I said a few that night and fell asleep dreaming of escape.

Morning came very soon and the shouting and unbolting of the doors signalled that a new life was beginning and I had better get used to it. Neither pyjamas nor night shirts were provided so I had to sleep in the shirt that I would wear for the rest of the week. Banging on the doors meant that prisoners had to be dressed and ready to exit their cell immediately the door was opened with their basin and pot to pour into a very large container that was carried around from cell to cell by the orderlies. This process was called 'slopping out'. Shaving was carried out always with cold water. I washed myself using the jug of water and basin that each cell contained and made up my bed. After receiving breakfast of porridge, tea, bread and margarine we, the latest arrivals, were locked up again as we had to be assigned our tasks by the Governor.

Later that morning we were individually marched into Governor Thompson's office in the main hall. Two warders marched at either side of me shouting 'left, right, march' and then 'stand to attention'. Thompson, who ruled the prison with an iron hand, gave me a lecture on prison discipline and the sanctions available to him before informing me that I was assigned to the tailors' workshop. Governor Thompson was never known to joke so I was amazed to hear that on the occasion of his retirement dinner in 1961 he raised the rafters with laughter when he said that his only regret of a lifetime of prison service was that 'I never got Donnelly back'.

On our return to A Wing I was shown the dining room which doubled as a recreation hall in the autumn and winter evenings. There I was given a plate, knife, fork, spoon and two mugs, one for milk for the porridge at breakfast and the other for tea. A locker space for these utensils was assigned to me along with instruction on the necessity to wash the utensils after each meal in one of the four large sinks. Community dining was the order of the day in A Wing, although a small number of prisoners were given permission to dine in their cells for various reasons.

The dining hall was full of tables and chairs to seat four persons per table. I was assigned to sit with Jim Devlin, a farmer sentenced to six years on the same day as me. Highly intelligent and very entertaining, Jim was great company. Later Frank Lanney from Castleblaney, serving three years for possession of a gun, joined our table. A married man with two children, he was fond of gardening and knew the name of every flower and plant in the garden we walked around in the mornings, winter and summer. There were eventually over 150 men who dined in that hall every day for breakfast, lunch and tea.

Some of our group were assigned to the cobblers' workshop and some to the tailors'. I could see the cobblers' counter from where I was seated as there was no barrier between the workshops – but tailors and cobblers could not mix. There were two prisoners side by side on each long bench. As tailors we sat with our legs outstretched and our backs to the wall. Later some of us were transferred to a tailors' workshop on the lower floor. An overcrowded facility whose walls ran with condensation when it rained, prisoners were usually sent to the 'snake pit' (as we called it) as punishment for some misdemeanour. I was sent there for refusing to carry large sacks of prison clothes from the tailors' workshop to the

A Wing gate. In fact, the result of this action was that no political prisoner thereafter was ordered to carry out that demeaning task. I considered this, in the scheme of things, a nice little victory.

Non-Political Prison Companions

We were treated by the authorities and prison staff as criminals. The Omagh Raiders, who were from Dublin and Cork, were unable to insist on political status and wore the uniforms from their first day in A Wing. Presumably their small numbers made any demand for political treatment unrealistic. We inherited their compromise. By wearing the prison garb we confirmed our criminal status in the eyes of the warders. Despite the growing numbers in A Wing, the Omagh Raiders managed to convince the incoming prisoners that they knew best and the criminal status endured by us was never really challenged.

Prison uniforms were made in our tailors' workshop. Brown uniforms were for short-term prisoners, those sentenced to less than two years. These prisoners were confined to B Wing. Blue serge tunics were worn by 'debtors', those who were unable to pay or who had neglected or refused to pay their lawful debts. Many of the prisoners from south of the border and some from the North found it unacceptable to socialise with ordinary criminals. They would ignore or barely acknowledge them and would certainly never sit with them by choice. They missed out on another world. I always regarded myself as a republican, a political prisoner, and all my correspondence from home invariably carried that description on the envelope for the world to see, particularly the prison authorities. However, I accepted the other prisoners as human beings who were not as fortunate as us. Their crimes usually deprived them of the respect of society generally, their neighbours in particular and often family members. We political prisoners enjoyed the respect of our families and that of most nationalists, even those who did not agree with our militant political stance. My parents' very inclusive attitude obviously had a real influence on me in this regard. It served me well later when planning my escape.

At first I was eager to learn how to sew when I saw some of our republican colleagues doing it so skilfully. Then there was the bonus that we could iron our hard linen striped shirts to make them more acceptable both in feel and appearance. Trying to coordinate feet and hands while using a Singer sewing machine was quite a challenge but came eventually after a lot of practice and expert advice. I regret to say, however, that my initial exuberance did not last long and my promising career as a Bond Street tailor ended almost as soon as it began. While we worked we enjoyed political discussions about the world, about Ireland and about what should be done as part of the ongoing IRA campaign. There were great debates on religion and the human experience. When we became overwrought with all that philosophical talk we had mini-concerts, when our little group would be joined by others from the other benches under the guise of teaching us how to perform some tailoring artifice. John Kelly would sing 'The Green Glens of Antrim' and others would recite a favourite poem. However, discussions and concerts were regularly broken up by the dour Mr Bell in charge of the tailors' workshop.

My Republican Colleagues – But Not in the Unit

Many of my fellow prisoners became very active again in later years when the Civil Rights movement was overtaken by state and loyalist violence. At the outset of the recent 'Troubles', John Kelly defended his own community in Belfast against attack and later became a leader in the Provisional movement. He was arraigned (and acquitted) on charges of attempting to import arms with fellow defendants, who included Neil Blaney and Charles Haughey, ministers in the Irish government. Prominent among the Provisional leadership in the 1970s were Daithí Ó Conaill and J. B. O'Hagan, who joined us in prison in 1959, while Kevin Mallon was very active also with the Provisionals. Seán Garland arrived in Crumlin Road shortly before Des O'Hagan was released, and both of them in later years held senior positions in what is loosely described as the 'official' republican movement, which struggled to oppose the growth of the Provisionals. There were about 100 long-term republican prisoners in Crumlin Road when I was there. Some I got to know well.

Something happened during my first days in A Wing which shattered my new world. On arrival, we learned through the grapevine that Tom Mitchell was the O/C in charge of prisoners, with Éamonn Boyce as Second-in-Command (2 I/C). Tom indicated that he wished to chat with me. My expectation was that he would explain the power structure and perhaps discuss his election campaign and the IRA campaign in Tyrone. He did none of these things. He explained to me in a kind of priestly confessional manner that he had a problem. Despite the fact that I had just received the longest sentence ever recorded for IRA membership, he told me that there was some opposition to me being allowed join the IRA unit in the prison. The reason given was that on the earlier charge of putting up posters I had recognised the court. I pointed out that if I had recognised the court on the IRA charge in October 1957 I would have had a separate trial and the most likely outcome would have been two years at most. Instead I had followed the standing IRA direction and paid dearly for it. The conversation was brief and I went to my cell dejected. How could he do this to me who had been so diligent and active during his three election campaigns and was, despite my young age, indispensable when it came to organising certain critical aspects? My service in the fight had been acknowledged by all, including the Lord Chief Justice, who retained his severest words of condemnation for me – and the longest sentence.

Tom never said who exactly objected nor did I ask; I wrongly assumed that it was a majority of the IRA prisoners in A Wing. In later years I discovered that most of the unit never heard about it so it was three people at most who made that decision. The basis for their decision was unfathomable and caused me great anxiety at a time when I had enough to worry about. I still cannot understand how older and more mature men could have dealt so harshly with a dedicated eighteen-year-old. Tom Mitchell and I never discussed the issue again. After my escape the IRA in Dublin were delighted to have me back and their welcoming press statement caused some consternation among that small minority in Crumlin Road.

Their refusal to have me in the prison IRA unit had personal ramifications not even considered at the time. Amazingly, it proved a watershed for me from which mostly good things sprang in the years ahead. Being a member of the prison IRA unit had very little tangible benefit as it was a fairly toothless body, but not being a member meant that I had no say in policy nor was I eligible for any office. I was outside the 'circle of trust'. There were psychological disadvantages, and incoming prisoners were told that I was not a member of the unit, indicating wrongly that it was my decision. Of course, I followed most of the unit's diktats and cooperated with their activities. Even though I was only a young lad, I took the view that if they didn't want me that was their loss. Ironically, not being a member of the unit enabled me to plan my escape without having to clear it with anyone.

The republican leadership in the mid-1960s included some of those ex-prisoners who put their own spin on history. From then on my successful escape was practically airbrushed out of the formal republican story to the extent that in 2007 the researchers for the newly established Crumlin Prison Museum could find no reference to my escape and therefore it was not included on the original timeline poster. This was rectified on my first visit to the prison. However, no revisionism of the period would prevent American historian Bowyer Bell from writing in his book *The Secret Army*:

Inside A Wing of Crumlin Road Prison Tom Mitchell, regularly re-elected as Prison O/C, proved capable of getting along with everyone and smoothing down the edges of faction. The problem of escape was not as vital in Crumlin, for beneath the great walls, topped with watch towers, and under the eyes of well-armed warders, a break seemed much more complicated than it did looking at the fields of Kildare through the strands of wire at the Curragh. Despairing of the official escape committee's lack of enthusiasm, most soon gave up hope. The old pre-campaign prisoners had accepted that they could not make it by themselves and GHQ was not going to help, despite all the floor plans and warder schedules smuggled out. A few did not give up so easily and against the most unlikely odds two even made a break. John Kelly with his Belfast contacts managed to smuggle in the proper tools at Christmas time 1960. Along with Dan Donnelly, who was not a member of the Crumlin IRA unit at the time, Kelly got on to the wall but slipped and fell into the yard below. Donnelly made it all the way, the only man to escape from Crumlin Road during the entire campaign. Inside the rest of the republicans realised that this one break was it and they would have to settle down and serve out their sentences. Most of the others had long since accepted that condition.

Despite their decision and my disappointment at being excluded from the unit I continued to be a loyal supporter of the fight for freedom. But Tom Mitchell's bombshell caused me to observe more critically the leadership at work in the prison and the type of personalities who were in the ascendant. As time went on no one ever came to me to question what had happened or discuss how best I could be 'reintegrated'. Nor did I ask. Not one of those who were clearly influential ever questioned Mitchell's decision. I made two decisions then. The first was that I was going to have all my school books brought in and I was going to put my time to good use; the second was that I would plan an escape.

London University: Crumlin Road Gaol Exam Centre

I wrote to London University and asked for details on what was required for the GCE (General Certificate of Education). They explained that I could sit each exam separately and that English was compulsory to obtain any certificate. Examinations were made available in spring and autumn. The university also confirmed that it was prepared to set up an Examination Centre for me alone if necessary. Prison censor Percy Noble read all letters and when he handed me this one he said that it would be necessary for me to write for permission from the Home Affairs Ministry to sit such an examination in the prison. Not long after receiving the letter from London University a leading member of the unit made it his business to walk around the yard with me one day at recreation. It was not hard to see that there was an agenda. He said he heard that I was considering applying for permission from the authorities to sit the London University examinations. He explained that it had never been done and that he and others were not in favour. I thought they had some cheek. I ignored their strictures and applied to sit the exams. The authorities, to their credit, approved the application immediately and in 1958 I sat my first London University exam.

It was the first time the university had nominated Crumlin Road Gaol as an exam centre. I encouraged many of the other prisoners to study and provided as much support as possible. I suggested that they select a subject and set out a study plan, and provided them with past exam papers that my brother Jim had obtained for me. I became an agent for promoting education and eventually the unit changed its tune and permitted members to seek permission to sit the GCE exams – including some of those who originally canvassed against such an initiative. The fact that I had sat and passed two GCE subjects in 1958 was widely publicised in the national papers.

Many prisoners then asked me about the process and the qualifications needed.

Before I left the prison as many as twenty prisoners (all
political) had either sat or were preparing to sit GCE exams in
a variety of subjects. The fact that many had very limited
technical or grammar school education (or none at all) made
their achievements all the more extraordinary and newsworthy.
It gave a meaning to their lives behind the grey walls and
provided an amazing confidence boost when they passed an
exam. All prospered in the years following their release.

In 1958 I passed the Irish Language paper and the English
Language paper. A lecturer from Queen's University Belfast
was allowed in to carry out the oral part of the Irish Language
exam in the chapel with two prison officers in attendance.
The following year a member of the French Consulate in
Belfast was employed by London University to carry out the
oral French exam with me under similar conditions. In 1959
and 1960 I successfully completed French, Latin, History and
English Literature, the latter two at advanced level, thereby
qualifying to register for the university's degree course.

How was this possible? There was a combination of
factors, the first being my excellent Christian Brothers
education. Another was that my final year school books were
brought to me in prison, which allowed me to continue
studying before I got out of the habit. A third was that a
neighbour of ours, Mrs Curry, sent me all of her late husband's
books. Michael Curry, a former teacher, had numerous books
he used for teaching with copious notes written in pencil
alongside almost every paragraph. These notes indicated wide
research and even wider reading on the subject. I marvelled at
his skill and competence. When I required books from the
library or other study material, my older brother Jim, who
worked in Pittman's Belfast at the time, made my requests a
priority and I am deeply indebted to him for his loyalty and
service during those years.

One of those who sat exams was Anthony Cooney from

Cork, arrested on the very first night of Operation Harvest with two others while preparing the attack on the RAF radar station at Torr Head. Anthony had planned a programme of education that centred on French and German. He obtained special permission to have a record player brought in so that he could listen to Linguaphone records and thereby improve his pronunciation. It was an incredible achievement as no radios, cameras, tape recorders or record players were ever allowed in to the prison. Anthony became fluent in both languages and later served the Irish export business with great distinction and with valuable benefits to Irish industry. Since I was studying French at the same time we helped one another increase our vocabulary. Fifty years later I received a small parcel from Germany with a note saying not to open 'until Monday'. The package contained a book – titled *French Fourth Reader* with my name written in the old Gaelic script, *Dónal Ó Donnghaile i gCarcéir Béal Feirste, Mí Iúil* 1958 (Daniel Donnelly in Belfast Prison, July 1958). I recognised it immediately, despite the years. Realising that I must have loaned it to Anthony I rang him in Germany. He said that when I loaned it to him he promised to return it 'on Monday'!

Everyday Living on A3

After a time I was moved to A3, which would be my home until my escape. My cell was number 13. In the row of cells alongside me were Paddy Devlin, Paddy O'Neill, Seán O'Neill and Fergus McCabe, all from Tyrone, and Frank and Éamonn Goodwin, Joe Owens and Harry Carson from Fermanagh. Éamonn Murphy and Eddie Mulholland were on A3 also. The latter two received the longest sentences handed down by any judge during the entire 1956–62 campaign. Having being captured in a dugout in east Tyrone with a veritable arsenal of weapons, they were given sentences of fifteen years each by Lord Justice Sheils, one of the few Catholic judges on the Northern Ireland Bench. Eddie was from Lurgan and Éamonn from Dublin. Eddie and I were very good friends in Crumlin

Road. He became a talented tailor and prided himself in his work. We often walked around the prison yard debating English literature, searching for rare words to challenge the depths of each other's knowledge. This was the kind of activity that shortened the days and made for interesting and enjoyable distractions from the drab life of the prison. Eddie was one of the last men to be released in 1963 and in later life became a published poet.

Life in prison was taking on a pattern that made it slightly more bearable. The upstairs tailors' workshop was warm and bright in those autumn days. Learning how to use the sewing machine was enjoyable, although the making of button holes less so as there was a real skill to it that no one could impart to me and quite frankly I wasn't sufficiently motivated. A pattern of activity entered my life which included reading and studying in my cell at night from seven o'clock to lights out at 9.30. Setting myself personal targets was a great exercise in reducing boredom and combating the routine of prison life. We went to the same workshop every day, went out for an hour's walk every morning whatever the weather. We ate the same food set out in a never-changing menu and always sat at the same table. Only for about two hours in the recreation period in the evening was there a change to the monotony. At this time we could circulate among different groups in the dining hall or in the yards in the summer.

The course of study I embarked upon gave great meaning to my day and was a sort of escapism when locked up in the evening. Reading and study broadened my mind and gave me a firmer basis for my own personal development. Reaching out to others as a result of this provided me with a growing confidence in my own ability.

I will never forget my first Christmas in prison, one of the worst experiences ever. Prisoners were allowed three parcels per year, at Easter, Hallowe'en and Christmas. They were, as you would expect, strictly prescribed – a certain amount of meat, a small cake, some sweets and a packet of biscuits. My mother included a large bottle of sauce to use with the roast beef. The censor informed me that the sauce was not allowed, and I had to give up the biscuits in order to be allowed keep it. The sauce was a lifesaver as I used it on bread to kill the taste of the obnoxious margarine. I would highly recommend sauce sandwiches.

We were allowed one letter per month and on occasion a letter from a relative or friend. Any other correspondence was either destroyed or kept in the office. If a prisoner knew that a letter had arrived for him and was not permitted to receive it he could ask for it to be given to his family on their next visit. At Christmas time a certain number of cards were allowed in but if they contained any political references either in the content of the card or written by the sender they were banned. I remember placing all my cards on the locker and reading them again and again. I particularly missed my three nephews, Eugene, Michael and Noel.

On Christmas morning Mass was said by Fr McAllister, the prison chaplain. Rosie was our organist and she loved to play the hymn 'Faith of Our Fathers' but some of the prisoners objected as it was written by an Englishman (even though it was played every year at the All-Ireland Finals in Croke Park up until the 1970s). The choir singing the traditional carols was a sharp reminder to me of the annual familial rituals that I was bitterly missing.

That Christmas there was a serving of sausages, the aroma of which was mouth-watering as we had neither seen nor smelt sausages since our first day of incarceration. Our anticipation of such a luxury was almost immediately deflated, however, by the fact that the sausages were sour and we had to dump them. The Governor later pledged that as we were such an ungrateful lot he would never again give us an 'Ulster fry'.

Christmas Day was like a Sunday; we were locked up for twenty hours out of the twenty-four to give the officers time to enjoy their own dinner and family gatherings. Thinking about Christmases at home, about visiting the crib in the church and then visiting friends, was a kind of relief – unless I thought too much about it. I was to celebrate Christmas three more times 'inside'.

Earlier in December the Governor permitted a concert in the chapel. It was a star-studded affair, opened by the Northern Ireland Light Orchestra and followed by Frank Carson who became a kind of a hero to us as he ignored the Deputy Governor's instructions to keep his act short. He and Jackie Wright, who later became famous through his appearances on *The Benny Hill Show* as the small baldy man who was the butt of Benny's jokes, came to the prison every year. They told the same jokes, which led to a Dublin man, Paddy Kearney, pledging that if one particular joke was told again he would shout out the punchline before the comedian could. An abridged version of the joke is that the bald comedian tells a story of losing his way while travelling to Whitehead in County Antrim. He eventually sees an old white-haired farmer working far away in a field, stops his car, climbs up on the ditch and shouts across, 'Whitehead?' while pointing with his finger in the direction he wished to have confirmed. Misunderstanding his gesture, the old man gives him the two-fingered salute while shouting back, 'Baldy'. It was a good joke. However, at the critical moment Paddy Kearney shouted out 'Baldy', destroying the comedian's story. Many of us were expecting this intervention so the laughing was loud while the comedian stood in seeming disbelief. Not for long, though, as Jackie Wright's training stood him in good stead, and like lightning he retorted, 'Are you still here?' which brought the house down.

Whenever anyone heckled Frank Carson he would look quizzically at the Governor and ask out loud, 'How did he get in?' and after a pause managed a double laugh with a question to us all: 'How the hell is he going to get out?' Fr McAllister also managed to bring in celebrities such as Freddy Gilroy and John Caldwell, Olympic boxing champions. I often wondered if they realised the enormous benefit we derived from their presence. They also did it free of charge, so whatever inconvenience and cost to them the benefit to us was a hundredfold. Their presence told us that people cared.

In prison you are stripped of your status and dignity. The regime, the shouted instructions, the affixing of a number which takes precedence over your name, the assignment to work, restrictions on movement, censored letters and controlled visits all combine to remind you that you are not master of your own destiny. There were some consolations, however, such as a newspaper delivered to my cell each day. You could select a paper and so I chose the *Northern Whig* which, alas, is no more. It was the oldest paper in Belfast and represented the unionist point of view. Most of my colleagues chose the *Irish News* and *Irish Press*, so I could swap my paper later that day. Thus I read two or three newspapers daily. Another pleasure was that every Saturday I received a bag of fruit consisting of two apples and two oranges supplied by the Prisoners' Dependents' Organisation. One day during the summer heatwave of 1959 I arrived back in my cell on a Saturday evening after recreation to find on my table a punnet of fresh strawberries with a layer of sugar melting on top. It was a most pleasant surprise but alas only happened once.

Until I started to write this book I was under the impression that every political prisoner received the weekly fruit parcel. Apparently this was not so. Prisoners who had recognised the courts were discriminated against. This was a mean-spirited decision by men who had no understanding of the fact that most of these young men were no less republican and patriotic than them, and maybe even more so. It is a great pity that this was never revealed as it would have been regarded as an outrage by most republican supporters who gave generous contributions out of meagre incomes without any such demarcation. Whether this was decided in Dublin or Belfast or within the prison is not clear, but certainly the prison's IRA unit leaders should not have permitted it.

8

EVENTS OUTSIDE AND INSIDE

In mid-November 1957 we learned of a terrible republican tragedy in a little cottage in Edentubber near the village of Ravensdale between Newry and Dundalk, close to the border on the Republic side. Five men were blown up by the premature explosion of a bomb they were preparing. The newspapers covered the funerals and appeals from Church and state for the campaign to stop. It was the lowest point, especially among prisoners, in the resistance campaign and cast a deep gloom over the entire wing. Jim Smith, whose cousin Paul Smith was one of those killed, was in A Wing with us serving eight years.

A major event in early 1958 was the trial of Francie Talbot and Kevin Mallon for the murder of Sergeant A. J. Ovens in a booby trap explosion at a vacant house in Brackaville near Coalisland, County Tyrone, the previous August. Several policemen and soldiers were injured in the attack. This event, no doubt, had influenced Chief Justice MacDermott when sentencing us. All of the signs were that Stormont was going for a guilty verdict and the death sentence for both men. Warders told us of the preparations being made in C Wing which housed the waiting cell and the gallows. We prayed day and night that they would not be executed. The republican leadership in Dublin, very sensibly, decided to break with tradition and agreed for the two men to be defended by one of the most eminent British lawyers, Elwyn-Jones, whose remarkable defence presentation resulted in a not guilty verdict. However, they were not released but held on lesser charges. Mallon was sentenced to fourteen years and Talbot to eight. It may seem a strange thing to say, but considering the alternative, we were very pleased to see them and they received a warm welcome into A Wing.

I got to know Francie Talbot well, a very pleasant man. I had just a nodding acquaintance with Kevin, who in later years became a leader in the Provisional movement. He was jailed in Mountjoy and Portlaoise at various times and managed with others to escape from both, the most daring being the famous 'helicopter escape' which greatly embarrassed Taoiseach Liam Cosgrave and Justice Minister Paddy Cooney.

At one point representatives of the Red Cross from Switzerland arrived to inspect Crumlin Road Gaol. The authorities were very concerned and actually locked up the bathing area; it was as if it never existed. The area, consisting of six baths and one shower, was a disgrace. There were designated bath days and a prisoner was entitled to a bath once a week. The day and time were not of our choosing. There were now several hundred prisoners in A Wing and it meant that bathing time for each was reduced to less than five minutes. The water was only lukewarm and privacy was almost non-existent. The most appalling aspect for me was that, bearing in mind that as many as twenty prisoners had been in and out of the bath before me, it had always a ring of scum which I had to remove before getting in. Without any cleaning fluid or real hot water it was an effort in futility as well as using up my bathing time. From our point of view the Red Cross visit was a flop. No political prisoner was interviewed as far as I know and no report ever published.

Then there was the 'stew crisis'. There was a set menu every week but occasionally there would be a change to the menu and this happened with a dish called 'stew', which was served on a Tuesday. To the amazement of myself and many others, an instruction was conveyed to the members of the IRA unit that the stew was to be boycotted as it was inedible. There was no explanation or discussion; it had been decided on high. I was always hungry in prison and going without dinner was a real sacrifice. Many others were of the same view. When dinner time came we all went into the dining room and took the container of stew from our tables and queued in single file to dump it in the bins. The result was that the stew was put on twice a week.

In reality the stew was no worse than the other food we were served and the boycott went on for months. Apart from the stew strike, I was always hungry in Crumlin Road Gaol. I was only eighteen and still growing. Although of poor quality the food was edible, but there was never enough of it. In my second year I went to the doctor to say that I was always hungry and wanted extra food. He just laughed and asked me was I serious. He told me that he would not approve any more regular food for me and that only the Governor could make such a decision. On demanding to see the Governor (having gone through quite a deal of bureaucracy), I was marched in the usual manner to his office where I made my request. There were two officers at each side of me and another behind me. I got no sympathy from the Governor; my request was denied.

I was never in the prison cookhouse but a prison officer who wrote about Crumlin Road twenty years after I left said that he never ate anything cooked there due to the infestation of rodents and cockroaches. One day in A Wing I was eating dinner when I noticed that the large dixie had animal faeces on the outside of the container. I immediately stopped eating and furiously upbraided the warder in charge of dinner distribution. I told the warders that I was putting my name down to see the Governor in the morning and I was also going to ask for permission to write to my local MP. After recreation that evening, my cell door was opened by Prison Officer Joe Boyd. He had a tray of tea and real roast beef sandwiches. Although he had nothing to do with the

cookhouse he was most apologetic and explained that because
of rodents in and around the cookhouse they needed a team
of cats, resulting in one of them leaving its mark on my
container. It was a meal to buy my silence. I enjoyed that feed
so much that I hadn't the heart to proceed further. Joe's action
saved somebody, as I am told the Governor had sacked people
before for less.

A Mission in a Prison

A real good talking point was the annual mission. Yes, in prison
someone thought that we could do with a mission to improve
our souls. A great character, the Franciscan Fr Lucius McClean,
came to us for a week, during which we had a daily service.
He was a breath of fresh air. Instead of preaching he asked us
to write out questions and he would answer them. He was
inundated with questions on theology, politics and philosophy.
He was a remarkable man and had a column in the *Sunday
Independent* which many of us read every week. He had the
common touch and could convince the hardest of us that
there is a God and that there will be a judgement day. Lucius
had a great sense of humour and no doubt wrote some of the
questions himself. One question he read out was: 'Father, what
is it like hearing the confession of nuns?' His reply was a
classic: 'It is like being snowballed to death.' He visited every
cell and spoke to every prisoner personally in A Wing.

Another missioner was the Dominican Fr Philip Pollock
from Belfast. He had served with the British forces during the
Second World War as chaplain. He was an effective preacher
but had no empathy with prisoners at all. Once from the altar
he told us that we should be very proud as Jesus was crucified
'between two of yourselves'. Of course, some of us considered
it very humorous to be compared to the two thieves but others
protested, resulting in the poor man having to apologise the
following day. The senior chaplain was Fr Paddy McAllister.
Highly regarded by the authorities, to me he appeared to be
uncomfortable among political prisoners. Nonetheless he did

wonderful work and many ex-prisoners could not praise him enough for the actions he had taken to improve their lot. Undoubtedly he was a most charitable man.

Fr McAllister asked every new penitent in confession why they were imprisoned, were they a member of the IRA and, if so, had they left the organisation. When I told him I was a member he refused to give me absolution, which, for a Catholic, is a serious obstacle to receiving Holy Communion. I was shattered by his refusal. It was a severe personal blow and it also had a depressing effect. After a period of time an assistant chaplain, Fr Timothy O'Regan, arrived from the Passionist Monastery in Ardoyne. He did not ask such questions and had the endearing habit of placing his hands over his ears when I told my sins. He always had words of encouragement for each prisoner and in my opinion was sent in especially to get Fr Pat off the hook and to hold on to this group of committed republicans as Catholics. The Catholic Church has not lasted 2,000 years without being pragmatic!

The Catholic hierarchy had taken a strong line against Operation Harvest, so the chaplain was just doing his job as he saw it. The bishops were against the Sinn Féin candidates in 1955, which was a natural follow-on from their opposition to any physical force campaign since the foundation of Maynooth College in 1795 when it was titled the Royal College and later funded by the British government. Like the Romans before them, the English had learned a thing or two about empires and decided to fund an educational college dedicated to turning out Catholic priests with an allegiance to the Crown and not to revolutionary ideas. The bishops were fiercely opposed to the republican forces in the Civil War (1922–3) and this aversion continued through to our times.

Growing up we were often reminded of the terrible denunciation uttered by Bishop Moriarty of Kerry who said, 'Hell is not hot enough nor eternity long enough for the Fenians.' In later years I participated on *The Late Late Show* with Gay Byrne, on a panel which also had a young Mary McAleese,

Michael Farrell of Civil Liberties fame and Richie Ryan, to
celebrate Seán MacBride's birthday. Before the programme I
was asked for my opinion on Archbishop Ó Fiaich's refusal to
condemn Sinn Féin. My reply was that Tomás Ó Fiaich was
first and foremost a historian and that he would have been
aware of Bishop Moriarty's condemnation and the fact that in
the centenary remembrance year of 1967 it was the Fenians
who were represented on the nation's stamp – and not Bishop
Moriarty. I was never invited back, even as a member of the
audience.

It is often asked why the Church did not suffer a falling-
off in support during these years. One reason may be that the
ordinary people had their own faith in God and despite a lack
of formal education could distinguish between their faith and
the political posturing of a clergy more in tune with the ruling
elite. In the election campaigns the Church authorities were
opposed to Sinn Féin candidates Philip Clarke and Tom
Mitchell in God-fearing Tyrone and Fermanagh, but that was
ignored by the electorate. As has often been the case in Ireland,
the people supported the Church when the Church was in
tune with their needs, and when it was not its directives were
ignored. Some of the older prisoners in Crumlin Road laid
the blame for the failure of the 1956 campaign on the
strictures imposed by the bishops. This is a fallacy. While it may
have had some effect on curtailing recruits in the South, it had
little effect in the northern counties. The real reason for the
campaign's failure was inept management and the lack of a
well thought-out, long-term strategy.

In prison most of us continued our morning and nightly
prayers with which we had been reared. The power of prayer
was a great solace to prisoners and made the whole experience
more bearable. Despite their dissatisfaction with the official
position of the Church, many continued to practise long after
they left prison. Their parents and a few well-disposed priests
can take the credit for that.

Republicans: South Versus North

Not being a member of the IRA unit in A Wing was a disadvantage in that I was not privy to what was going on between GHQ in Dublin and us prisoners nor did I know the topics of current debate between them. Already the arrest and conviction of Seán Garland and J. B. O'Hagan in December 1959 and later Daithí Ó Conaill in March 1960 had introduced heavyweights into the inner politics of A Wing. Garland received four years for the same charge as me – membership of the IRA. Ó Conaill and O'Hagan, ambushed by the RUC in County Tyrone, were seen as the most active IRA men in the North.

Daithí Ó Conaill, our training officer before the campaign began, was brave beyond a doubt and had the intelligence to support it. Of all the people held in Crumlin Road Gaol he was one of a very few capable of masterminding an escape. J. B. O'Hagan lived a very full life and was jailed in Crumlin Road as a young man in the 1940s and again in the 1950s. He was also interned in the Curragh in 1958 and saw the inside of Mountjoy Gaol in Dublin on several occasions. He was a gigantic figure in the republican movement over many years and became an iconic leader during the Provisionals' more recent armed struggle. During the thirty years' war his wife, Bernadette, was jailed in Armagh Women's Prison on a concocted charge and his sons were sentenced to long terms in Long Kesh during the same period.

There was perceptible tension manifested by the visible unease of the old order. For the most part the southern political prisoners socialised together, and to my mind a certain superiority emanated from them towards the local prisoners. On average they were about a decade or so older than us and generally had a better education. Many of them made no effort to welcome newcomers to the wing. They walked with one another and seldom engaged in any kind of debate with the rest of us. The men from the South were in charge of A Wing and considered it their right. Ideas or opinions that did not conform to their view were not readily accepted.

There were only a few Belfast men in A Wing, due mainly to the fact that there had not been a single incident of note in Belfast during the 1950s campaign. D Wing, however, which was reserved for political prisoners whom the government considered had either acted or were about to act against the interests of the British regime, was full of Belfast men. John Kelly, arrested in Dunamore, County Tyrone, as leader of an active service unit, was one of the few Belfast men in A Wing. Although highly respected by everyone, he was deprived of a leadership position within the wing by the subtle promotion of a southern prisoner when he stood for election as O/C.

Belfast republicans had come through the scorching white heat of the sectarian crucible that physically destroyed many lives, forced humiliating living conditions on them and deprived most of an opportunity to work. They had their own black humour and a steely determination to outwit the Unionist oligarchy that controlled and managed the affairs of the Six Counties to their own advantage. The benefit of this experience was never utilised by those who controlled the prisoners in A Wing. What we had instead was an elite who circulated the many benefits they enjoyed among themselves, for example a radio, recently published books on Irish republican history and the *United Irishman* newspaper, which was smuggled in to the prison. Those like myself who sold hundreds of copies of this paper on a monthly basis even though it was banned in the North never saw sight of it in all the years we were inside.

The republican movement was and is a living example of the tendency for Irish organisations to split. The 1916 Rising was almost aborted because of such a split when Eoin MacNeill directed Volunteers through the national papers to ignore Pádraig Pearse's call to arms. This resulted in only a small number of areas rising up. The worst split of all occurred six years later when the Treaty was signed, plunging the country into Civil War, while the 1920s and 1930s saw a further diminution of the movement with the expulsion of much of the intellectual talent who wanted the movement to pursue a more socialist programme in line with the declaration of the First Dáil in 1919. The Second World War years, which saw the beginning of a bombing campaign in Britain, resulted in another split – those in favour and those against. This particular campaign was a disaster and the bitter split between comrades in the first Curragh Camp made a resurrection seem impossible. During that period de Valera's government executed several IRA men while others were allowed to die on hunger strike.

The rebirth of the movement in the late 1940s and 1950s was an unbelievable achievement. The names mostly associated with this are Tony Magan, Tomás MacCurtain and Pádraig McLogan, who built, with the support of many other very committed people, an organisation that managed to carry out successful raids on British Army barracks in Ireland and England and succeeded in having two Sinn Féin MPs elected to Westminster and four TDs to Dáil Éireann. Even then, however, there were splits, with the emergence of groups such as Liam Kelly's Saor Uladh and Joe Christle's Dublin faction. The movement managed to retain its shape and leadership, however – until internment in the Curragh began in 1957. At one stage in 1958 there were 180 prisoners, including many of the leaders of the republican movement, detained there without trial.

Those who had brought the movement from tatters to its extraordinary pre-eminent position in the 1950s considered the organisation their own property and ruled it with a certainty and experience that brooked no dissent. Younger prisoners in the Curragh were frustrated first by their imprisonment without trial and then by the realisation that their role in the campaign was at an end before it even began. This frustration was magnified by the apparent lack of any coherent plan of escape by those in charge. But the leadership was opposed to any attempted escape that could result in death or serious injury either to prisoners or jailers.

On 2 December 1958, however, an incident occurred that would lead eventually to yet another split. Sixteen IRA prisoners cut the barbed wire around the prison camp and escaped, in contravention of the leadership's instructions. It was a great coup for the IRA, of course, but a dismayed leadership demanded that the escapees be court-martialled. One of these escapees, a very popular young man named Gerry Haughian from Lurgan, later arrived in Crumlin Road Gaol having being captured and sentenced to nine years' imprisonment. At an IRA Army Convention, however, those involved had their unofficial action approved in a Jesuitical judgement when they were first discharged from the IRA and then immediately allowed to reapply. The result was a further weakening of the movement and the loss of people of the calibre of Magan, MacCurtain and McLogan and many others. While there may have been personal divisions and minor power struggles, the real reason, of course, was that Operation Harvest had been defeated. Victors celebrate but the vanquished turn on one another. In more recent times we have seen the Provisional and Official split of the 1970s and the fragmentation of those into groups like the INLA (Irish National Liberation Army) and more latterly, with less impact, the emergence of the Real IRA and Continuity IRA.

Lack of success is usually a prerequisite for a split; people like to be associated with success. The republican movement, as it developed, made principles out of tactics. It struck a pose before history and ignored the reality of ordinary folk. For example, most people regarded the Dublin government as legitimate by virtue of a succession of general elections in the twenty-six counties but for decades, on a point of principle, the republican movement refused to recognise the Dáil. People generally were too preoccupied with eking out a living to be overly concerned with such issues.

Although the division in the Curragh Camp had no

immediate effect on us in A Wing, it was not happening in a vacuum. In that strange way of human nature, the effects would be seen in another generation. The beginning of the division between northern and southern republicans could be seen in Crumlin Road in the 1950s. There were not enough northerners there who were prepared to debate the real issues such as the future for the republican movement. Éamonn Timoney from Derry was one such man of clear vision and an independent mind. His jousts with some of those from the South were harbingers of a future time when those domiciled in the Six Counties would effectively take control of the leadership. Their ability to seek solutions based on practicalities over established principles has achieved massive electoral support and real governmental power with a minimum of division.

9

PLANNING THE BREAKOUT

Keeping an Eye on the Outside

Our time in Crumlin was brightened by news of the Curragh breakout in December 1958 and the subsequent escape by Daithí Ó Conaill and Ruairí Ó Brádaigh from the Curragh just six months before the Fianna Fáil government closed the internment camp. Another escape that gladdened the heart was that of Séamus Murphy from Wakefield Prison in England in February 1959. He and two others were serving life sentences for a raid on Blandford Army Barracks in which tons of ammunition were taken. The men in British prisons were constantly on our minds. What kind of life did they have among seasoned criminals who had neither an understanding nor sympathy for their cause?

During my years inside, the international news that made most impact on us was the death of Pope Pius XII. And what a surprise his successor, 83-year-old Pope John XXIII, had in store in the five years of his pontificate. The election of John Fitzgerald Kennedy, the first Catholic president of the US, in November 1960 was another milestone. And extraordinary as it may appear to younger readers, the victory of Fidel Castro and the ousting of the dictator Batista in Cuba was greeted as warmly by us in prison as Kennedy's election. Castro's ascension to power brought land reform, education and health for Cuba's poor. His forces' military campaign featured many of the guerilla tactics favoured by the IRA and we were, therefore, their natural allies.

The long battle for independence and freedom in Kenya, led mainly by the Kikuyu ethnic group, came to an end in 1960 with the declaration by the British of an end to the 'emergency'. The Mau Mau were defeated militarily but most of their demands for land reform and democracy had been conceded, although at a terrible price. This war had begun in 1952 and again the nationalist Irish sided with the Mau Mau despite the usual smear tactics of the British press, both gutter and high brow. Over 50,000 people were killed and the British executed over 900 men during that period. Even before I was jailed I used to read with horror of the torture and killings by the British military. Interestingly, we were indebted to *Time* magazine as its reporters often told the stories of the 'underdog', even if it had an imperial slant. I received the magazine regularly. Irish newspapers, on the other hand, took all their international news from Reuters or Associated Press which meant that one had to read a cross-section of newspapers and even then read between the lines to obtain some semblance of what was really happening. The real horror of Kenya was uncovered with the massacre of eleven African prisoners in a concentration camp known as the 'Hola Camp', a name forever associated with torture and death – and with the British.

British Prime Minister Harold Macmillan made a famous speech in which he spoke of 'the winds of change' blowing through Africa. The winds were blowing well before he noticed them but at least his statement showed that at last there was a recognition of the need to concede to the Africans the right to rule themselves. It would take another thirty years and a lot of bloodshed before the British would take heed of the winds of change blowing in a small island not too far away.

In Cyprus, meanwhile, the Greek majority sought union

with mainland Greece in a war against the British through their version of the IRA called EOKA. They had begun an armed struggle under the leadership of Colonel Grivas and had succeeded in waging a very successful war against British troops until a ceasefire was agreed in April 1959 and eventually an independent Cyprus. We were ecstatic at the peace developments which indicated that Britain, after waging a bloody war, losing many soldiers and having executed thirty-eight EOKA members, again bowed to the inevitable that their day was over. We were envious of EOKA's success compared to our achievements or lack thereof.

Another constant topic of conversation and debate was Israel. We were well informed of its history and admired the Israelis' achievements in economics and the restoration of Hebrew as a spoken language. The general consensus among us was that any future guerilla war in the Six Counties should be based on the strategy and tactics of the Irgun, a Jewish outfit designed to establish a homeland for the Jews in Palestine. We listened to the telling and retelling of how the Irgun had brought the fight to the British during their Protectorate rule. The bombing of the King David Hotel in 1948, when forty soldiers were killed, was regarded as a major blow to the British and contributed greatly to the eventual setting-up of the state of Israel. Here again Jewish fighters and ex-prisoners lived to be elected to high office, such as Menachem Begin of the Irgun who eventually achieved the office of Prime Minister. The exploits of the risen Jews in their new land gave us hope for an Ireland free and Gaelic.

Another major event that caused much grief was the Niemba Ambush in the Congo in November 1960 where nine Irish soldiers were brutally killed by members of the Baluba tribe. It was a real setback for the Irish Army's peacekeeping role internationally. The soldiers were from Dublin and the story held the headlines for days on end. Here again we could identify with the Congolese against the colonial power of the Belgians and the horrendous exploitation of the natives by the Belgian rubber companies.

A struggle similar to our own was the fight between the FLN and France in Algeria. France regarded Algeria as an integral part of Metropolitan France and therefore its own national territory. Like the British in Ireland, many thousands of French citizens had been planted in Algeria with a view to ruling it forever in the name of France. During those years the French and British vied with one another as to who could design the most innovative form of torture of political prisoners and who could perpetrate the most dastardly atrocity. Ben Bella was imprisoned from 1958 to 1962 before becoming Prime Minister of the independent Algeria. He was in prison around the same time as we were in Crumlin Road. We fought for the same principles – the freedom of our country and the right to rule ourselves.

All of these events saw the challenging of colonial masters in various parts of the world. They demonstrated that nationalism was on the rise and that people everywhere were awakening to demand their rights. As political prisoners we were always on the side of the underprivileged. We were at one with those fighting the French colonial power in Algeria, the Greek Cypriots in Cyprus and the Mau Mau in Kenya, the latter two against the British. The lessons for Ireland were recognised by many of us in Crumlin Road. The world is a very different place now but the international ferment of the time was echoed in the Six Counties by our own – albeit comparatively mild – struggle.

New Order in A Wing and Thoughts of Escape

Within a year of arriving in A Wing Seán Garland replaced Tom Mitchell as O/C of the unit. Mitchell apparently stood down and Garland was elected in October 1960 unopposed. Many northerners had a lot of experience and had shown an interest in the job on previous occasions but were not proposed. It was the manifestation of a view that a prisoner from north of the border could not be trusted with the job and may well have been a directive from GHQ in Dublin whose company Seán would have enjoyed more recently than any of the other prisoners. This happened just three months before I escaped. There was a general consensus that Seán would raise morale despite the insipid ongoing campaign, and indeed he attempted to do so by creating another new escape committee whose task it was to identify a route out. He did not ask me to participate. In fact I never knew the committee existed until I raised the issue with John Kelly. Seán Garland only held the position for a year. After I escaped he was succeeded by a Derry man named Liam Flanagan, a very popular man and a latecomer to the prison. It is reported by Éamonn Boyce that he and Seán Garland were appalled by this election result.

Since my imprisonment I had dreamed of escaping. On smoggy days I wondered if I could climb the outer wall during the period the warders would count and re-count to establish if anyone was missing. You have no idea, unless you lived in Belfast at that time, how dense and choking the November smog was. At an early stage I discounted many apparently good ideas as they mostly fell down on the one great hurdle – how to reach the top of the wall without being spotted by the armed police in the gun towers. No matter how I imagined it, the only chance of not being seen would be during a smog. But of course, however frequent it may have been, the smog was not forecastable, and in addition there was the problem of scaling the wall.

Then came the security review. To my delight they began to build a higher wall. The missing part of my jigsaw for escape was put in place when the authorities raised the low link wall (from the administration block to the outer wall) to the same level as the outer wall. As I went through every possible scenario it was clear to me that I needed a companion. At various times I chatted with particular prisoners whom I regarded as ideal comrades for such a venture. However, the all-encompassing security of the place was such that none of them thought there was much of a chance. Of course, I could not reveal much to other prisoners as it was all academic at this stage, so there was no specific proposal from me. In any case, I did not receive enough positive reaction to take anyone at that stage into my confidence.

A major issue for me was how to get out of Belfast without detection. Another was where to go in the event of a problem arising. I concluded, therefore, that my best possible ally would be a Belfast man, although there were not too many in A Wing. John Kelly was one, however, and he and I began to share a table in the dining room at this time. John was a particularly well-liked man, both on his own account and because of his family history and his family's contribution to the welfare of prisoners and their families. They lived very near the prison, just off Crumlin Road. John was a born leader with an innate ability to get on with everyone. His brother Billy was interned in D Wing without trial and was still being held there at this time. The family had a fruit wholesale and retail business in the Markets which did a roaring trade. Every prisoner who was released from Crumlin Road was given the Kellys' address, 12 Adela Street, to which they were directed. Many of those who took up the invitation still talk about the welcome they received and the generosity of the Kelly family. John had been arrested in Dunamore, a mountainy area of Tyrone near Cookstown, in December 1956 and therefore saw little action in the actual campaign despite all his training. John and I had been part of the discussion and mini-concert group in the upper tailors' workshop (the proper one). I knew his character fairly well and considered him an ideal comrade for the escape project. He was a member of the IRA unit and was also a member of the official unit escape committee set up by Seán Garland.

I knew John well enough to ask him when there would be an official escape. His answer confirmed what I had already presumed: 'They will never escape.' Apparently many floor plans of the prison, timetables of warders' movements and recommended actions had been smuggled out to GHQ in Dublin without ever receiving a positive response. In fairness to GHQ and their advisers within Crumlin Road, an escape was a long shot and did not appear possible under most circumstances.

During a period of recreation in summer 1960 while we sat in the garden yard in the evening I told John I had a plan and asked if he would be interested in helping to expand and implement it. He agreed immediately. I was delighted as I now had a Belfast man on board and, more importantly, a highly intelligent and creative mind. An added bonus was that John was housed in A2, the middle floor, whereas I was in the 'penthouse' in A3 and my cell was directly above his. First we created a code so that when we spoke about our planned escape no one would recognise the subject. While we took care not to be overheard, we were paranoid about new technology that enabled the 'spooks' to listen in to conversations. We discussed how John's unit pals would react but he demonstrated his independence by declaring that if we were successful it would be a great feat for political prisoners at a time when there was very little cheer. He added that even by attempting an escape we would be maintaining a tradition among republicans in every phase of the struggle for independence. He considered the plan to be realistic and well worth a try. We were on our way.

We set a few ground rules. We would commit nothing to paper, for security reasons. In the Operation Harvest campaign and later, many IRA documents were seized by the RUC and Gardaí that compromised actions. In addition, we would take no one else into our confidence until we were both of the same mind. We followed this methodology scrupulously, with the result that the secrecy of our project was protected until the last day. The most difficult aspect was not talking about our plans except when necessary. We were both tailors but in different shops and we walked around the yard in the mornings with different prisoners. Our opportunities for discussion were quite limited, confined to the recreation periods in the evening after tea. In the summer months it was easier since we were outdoors, whereas in the winter we were confined to a relatively small, busy and noisy dining hall.

The basics of the plan dealt with the best time to attempt an escape and the most advantageous place to start. The idea was to cut through the bars of a cell to access the yard where the outer wall is nearest the actual Crumlin Road. Using this as a starting point meant that it would give us a choice of times within a restricted timeframe. The next step was the making of the rope, some 70 feet long, to stretch from an anchored spot on the administration block across the new link wall and down the outer wall which we reckoned was about 30 feet high. The challenge here was that at a certain spot on the link wall and for the last 10 yards we would be in full view of the armed police in the gun towers while crossing. Therefore we planned to be less than ten seconds on that part of the wall so that even if we were spotted the chances of them taking up their weapons and firing in that space of time were fairly remote. This may seem a rather cavalier attitude, but there were two elements in our favour. One was that there had never been even an attempted escape in the four years the gun towers were *in situ*; the other was that we would have the element of surprise and would be on the wall at night time when they depended on their heavy-duty spotlights. The plan continued in its framework form to include an outside party of Belfast republicans to whisk us away either across the border via south Armagh if we escaped unnoticed or to a safe house in or around Belfast.

Then we got down to the detailed planning. We had to decide a time frame and agree an exit date. I had chosen Christmas Eve as the most suitable date, for a number of reasons. There would be thousands of shoppers in the city, which would make things very difficult for the security forces both in terms of spotting an escaped prisoner and attempting to stop and question members of the public as they rushed around town. Another benefit was that within the prison there would be a degree of excitement due to prison visits, while domestic pressure on prison officers would also create a distraction from security matters. As a 21-year-old I also had a romantic historical reason for choosing the date as it was on Christmas Eve that Red Hugh O'Donnell escaped from Dublin Castle in 1592. Interestingly, Pádraig MacGiolla, the Donegal-born editor of the *Ulster Herald* newspaper based in Omagh, wrote following my escape: 'Young Donnelly, whose daring dash from the prison fortress, which is heavily guarded by patrols and machine gun nests, made the biggest news of the Christmas season in the Six Counties, escaped in a manner that recalled Red Hugh O'Donnell's Christmas breakout from Dublin Castle centuries ago.'

The framework plan was then broken down to individual components under the headings 'timing' and 'materials'. The exit point was John's cell on A2 as it constituted a lower drop to the ground. We both studied again the outer bars of thick steel and also the aluminium-type frame that housed the sixteen panes of glass and which was sealed into the brickwork of the window. That would have to be cut also. Cutting the bars and the window frame presented us with a massive challenge. It would probably take more than one day to cut the bars, and if there was any unexpected delay we would have to conceal the cuts from any warder carrying out a visual inspection. So we needed to identify how they could be cut while leaving the frame to obscure the selected bars. An added requirement, of course, was that we had to create a large enough aperture for us to climb through. We had all evening until lights out and, more particularly, most of every Sunday when we were locked up for twenty hours out of the twenty-four to think about it. Afterwards we would meet and discuss our findings.

The bars to be cut were identified and also the corresponding window frame. They needed to be cut at an angle to achieve a certain cover for the outer bars when cut. I managed this by practising every night in my cell for about a fortnight at climbing through the smallest aperture possible. This was done by sticking a very strong rolled-up magazine in a vertical position on the floor under the horizontal iron of the bed frame. The magazine chosen was *Paris Match*, which I received regularly to help with my French studies. The magazine was made from thick, high-quality paper and when rolled up was almost as strong as a light piece of wood. I would lie on the floor at the bottom of the bed and crawl under the bed frame which was about a foot from the floor and then attempt to exit the opening between the magazine and the leg of the bed at the bottom. When I succeeded in this I would then move the magazine to reduce the space and try again. This was done over several weeks as we both worked on a keep fit regime by using the calisthenics we learned at school. When I had achieved my best result I gave the magazine to John and the measurements of the smallest aperture for him to practise and achieve, which he did. It did not matter mathematically where the bars were cut as long as we could get out through the hole, but it was a major concern that the cuts should be made where they could be disguised to prevent detection. We intended to use chewing gum or putty for this purpose. This was an important step in our planning and as we checked off the list of preparatory things to be done, it increased our belief in being able to pull it off.

Procurement Issues

Our next task was to identify the source of a 70-foot rope. Just at this time, outside electrical contractors were busy in A Wing installing fluorescent lighting which in the 1950s was considered a great technological advance. The contractors were also charged with the task of installing new lights on the outer wall of A Wing. These contractors worked in the prison under strict security and under specific restrictions which, if breached, would result in dismissal or loss of contract. They worked under the watchful eye of a trade officer who knew about construction, electrical work and other skills, and their time in the wing was structured so that they would only be there when the prisoners were at work or recreation. Before long I identified a possible source of materials for making the rope. There were large reels of electric flex used for wiring the new lights, and I figured that these, bound and entwined with my two sheets or blankets torn in strips, would make a fine rope. John and I discussed this possibility and agreed that it was our best bet. We had looked around for other materials in the hope that some of the tradesmen may have used a rope that we could 'borrow', but no such luck. When we returned from the workshops the contactors and their equipment were usually gone, all part of the tight security precautions.

Hiding things in a prison is almost impossible and trying to hide something for any period of time simply cannot be done. It was agreed that I should acquire as much electric flex as possible before the contract was finished, and by asking innocent questions about how long such a contract would normally last I established the latest date possible for taking some material. Coming back one day to the wing after a visit I saw that the workmen were active as it was not yet dinner time. I suggested to the accompanying warder that it was not worth while going back to the workshop as it was almost one o'clock. He agreed and brought me to my cell. Part of the standard equipment in a cell was a jug and basin, and we were always allowed to have a jug of water. To avoid being locked up immediately I requested permission to fetch a jug of fresh water from the tap at the end of the corridor. As I strolled along I observed the workmen busy with threading the wire through the roof space and into the wall cavities that concealed the wiring. Also observed were the positions of the materials and equipment. There on the corridor were two reels of electric flex, one new and the other half used. I had brought both my jug and basin, as we often took a basin of water for washing to save the jug of water for drinking. Taking my time filling the jug, I saw that the supervisor and trade warder were engaged in a technical discussion. Stopping to look and to admire the neat workmanship, I placed my empty basin on the floor close to the electric flex. As the workmen and others became engrossed in the work at hand I quickly placed the half roll of wire in the basin and nonchalantly walked back, ensuring that the jug full of water concealed the contents of the basin. On reaching my cell I was fortunate that the officer had gone to the desk at the centre of A3, and once inside I placed the roll of wire under the chamber pot in the corner behind the door until I could find another hiding place. The workmen would no doubt notice the roll missing and would search for it or assume that they were either mistaken or that other workers had brought it to the lock-up store. If they searched and found it in my cell I would claim that I was just placing it out of harm's way. After dinner I would have to find a more effective hiding place until it was required.

Next on our list of things to procure were hacksaw blades to cut the bars. There were several issues for us to consider. How were we to get a message out to someone we could trust and how could the blades be smuggled in? And if we did manage it, where would we hide them? Being found with electric flex was one thing – the discovery of hacksaw blades in your cell quite another. Having established the how, where and who, we decided not to import them until nearer the date. John was a marine fitter engineer by trade and so had practical experience of cutting equipment and how best to use it. Consequently, he took responsibility for procuring the hacksaw blades.

He informed me, in code, that the blades would be arriving by the desired date. This was a critical event in the implementation of the escape. I never asked who was supplying them or how; I knew that John was an expert at delivering the goods. My job would be to hide them safely. In order to bind my books I was allowed a small roll of Sellotape in my cell, so when the blades arrived I taped them to the underside of the locker where I kept my books.

Unannounced personal and cell searches were a common feature. I considered that I was subject to more frequent searches than any other prisoner in A Wing and had made an official complaint, but to no avail. My purpose in complaining was to encourage them to desist from frequent searches as our project would soon be in a critical phase. The standard practice was to take three prisoners at a time from their work and lock them in their cells. Two warders would then go from cell to cell carrying out a forensic search. The prisoner would have to take off his clothes and boots, which would be searched for contraband, weapons or anything else unusual. The warder would feel around the stitching and edging to make sure nothing was hidden. Everything in the locker was also thoroughly scrutinised.

Around this time I was called out of the workshop with two others for the usual search. On entering my cell I sat on the edge of the bed opposite the locker and bent down to untie my shoelaces. To my horror I saw one of the blades hanging loosely from its position under the locker. The heat in the pipes running through the cell had dried out the Sellotape. I had to act swiftly as I heard the warders approach. I had no option but to use another piece of tape to stick the blade back up. I had just done it and was back on the bed trying to look calm when the two entered. One immediately asked for my clothes while the other got down on his knees to look under the locker. I could not believe it; I thought they were on to something. He quickly changed position, however, and began to take out my books, at which point I breathed an inward sigh of relief.

In the event, John found the blades useless for the purpose as they were too small and we had no handle to attach to them, so he had to go again and attempt to procure larger blades. This he did, and by now I had found a much safer place for them – a slight weakness in the steel frame of my bed. I inserted them and camouflaged the job with black polish. Then we decided to keep them in our possession during the working day so in the tailors' workshop I made a little cloth satchel for them. This allowed one of us to carry them in a trouser leg at all times and facilitated handover if called out to be searched.

10

ESCAPE!

One of our concerns was that we did not know how the front of the prison had changed as a result of the recent security work. We could hear work being carried out but could not see what was happening. Another major question concerned the habits of the warders when they went on and off duty. Did they hang around in groups chatting, for example? Neither did we know how often the warders carried out their security round behind the walls of the tailors' workshop, vegetable garden and hospital area or how they communicated to the control tower. To all these questions it was my job to find the answers.

From the awful smog that winter I had acquired a bad dose of bronchitis. Dr McComb, the resident prison doctor, had no sympathy with prisoners and regarded us all as malingerers, no matter how infrequently you visited him. When I went to him about my persistent bronchitis I was given one of his infamous bottles of medicine that was not much better than coloured water. I complained to him about its inefficacy but he just dismissed me with another bottle. Within a few days my mother came to visit and commented on the bad cough. During those visits we developed a kind of telepathy whereby I could communicate with her without having to spell it out. A passing reference to our GP in Omagh, Dr James McMullan, was enough. The following week I was

called to the Governor's office. He was incensed that Dr
McMullan had written to the authorities officially
complaining of the poor medical attention afforded to me in
A Wing and demanding permission to come to the prison to
examine me. He informed me, not surprisingly, that Dr
McMullan would not be allowed in under any circumstances,
before referring me back to Dr McComb. It was probably
McComb's first time to be held accountable for anything in
Crumlin Road. The upshot of this little contretemps, however,
was that I was scheduled for an X-ray in the Royal Victoria
Hospital. Now I would have an opportunity to see the inner
yard in front of the locked gates and also the outside of the
prison.

On the appointed day I was escorted by three prison
officers through the administration block and placed in
handcuffs. To my great disappointment I saw that they were
bringing me in a Black Maria, which meant that my only
chance of seeing out was through the small window up high.
Three uniformed policemen and one plainclothes detective
were inside the van, while a car containing four plainclothes
detectives followed behind. Inside the van I spoke amiably and
told them that I had not seen the outside world for three and
a half years. With that I stood up and looked out the little
window. The two policemen handcuffed to me also stood up,
which allowed me to take a good look at the front of the
prison as we drove out. This happened two weeks before we
escaped.

The hospital waiting room was cleared out for my arrival,
and the bemused doctors and nurses were finding any excuse
to come and peer in at this manacled man. They had to uncuff
me to allow for the X-ray and for a few minutes I found
myself without the police and was very tempted to try an
escape, even though I had no idea of the geography of the
hospital. On the journey home I got another peek out of the
window and confirmed the layout outside the prison. Taking
my time while exiting the van in the open space inside the

gates provided me with a clear knowledge of the improvements made and the obstacles we faced. Another task checked off.

The warders would sometimes discuss the education of their children with me and ask advice. This was after newspaper reports of my academic achievements while inside. As part of these conversations I would ask seemingly innocuous questions that would not raise suspicion. For example, our selected time for exiting the prison via the outer wall coincided with a change of guard, and we were genuinely concerned that groups of warders would be hanging around in groups chatting. 'I suppose you all have a chat on the Crumlin Road after work when you leave the prison,' I'd enquire. The answer was reassuring: 'That area is clear within ten seconds, we can't wait to get home.' In a similar manner I compiled information regarding their walking security checks in the evening and at night as they passed out of sight behind the tailors' workshop.

John and I agreed that we would leave the cutting of the bars and window frame until as late as possible to minimise the risk of a window check by the warders. One officer had the disconcerting habit of going into every cell when working as class officer, standing on the head of the bed and striking the bars in several ways to ensure their integrity. He did this while we were at the workshop. On 23 December John and I asked our respective class officers for permission to give our cells a thorough cleaning. This meant washing the walls and floor and scrubbing the table and locker. A lot of water was required, which then had to be disposed of in the sluice room and this necessitated a lot of walking back and forth to the tap and the disposal area. Always keen to encourage cleaning, the authorities facilitated both of us. As we had chosen John's cell as the exit point, he began the process of sawing the bars. We agreed to saw the outer bars first and leave the window frame last as the frame would obscure the saw marks on the bars. The plan was that I would take my table out on to the

corridor and scrub like hell while John made his first attempt
at cutting the bars. It was a nerve-wracking operation as both
class officers stood at the official desk in the middle of the
respective levels. On a pre-arranged pattern I would scrub hard
and as loudly as possible and then before stopping completely
would lower the volume to indicate to John that he could rest.
Our ability to synchronise was of paramount importance.

After a period I requested permission to go to John's cell
for something. He had made substantial progress, despite
having to use the blades without the benefit of a blade holder.
As a result his hand was scoured, both by the movement of
the bare blade and the awkward position that had to be
maintained at the window. We eventually made a kind of
handle for the blade to minimise the pain. For a short period
he took his table out to the corridor while I remained in his
cell and gave him a well-earned break. This could only work
for a while before I had to return to my own cell to avoid
suspicion. While we had made progress, it was much slower
than we anticipated. My table was well scrubbed and the class
officer more or less told me that it was clean enough. The
noise was probably annoying him. This made it necessary for
us to seek additional help, which we got from an unusual
source. A Belfast man imprisoned for theft had been working
as an orderly on John's landing. Both John and I had always
greeted him and indeed shared some of our Christmas parcels
with him, not realising that our good deed would be returned
some day. I asked him, without fully disclosing our plans, to
scrub some of the tables nearer to John's cell to create sufficient
noise as cover. It was a risk, but one that paid off. As an
ordinary criminal he would have benefited well from exposing
us, but he was as efficient and loyal as any republican Volunteer.

At times like this one appreciates the common thread of
humanity and how every person, no matter their
circumstances, should be treated with dignity. I am forever
grateful to him as his contribution, although minor, was vital
to our plan. During this duet between table and bars I

wandered up to the A2 class officer to chat with him and divert his attention. As we chatted I noticed that he was uneasy, and was concerned that he had noticed something and was waiting his moment. I stayed with him as long as was appropriate before signalling to John to cease the operation. John used putty and chewing gum to fill in the cuts in the bars before colouring them with black polish. It looked increasingly likely that we needed more time and that our Christmas Eve escape would be delayed.

Later the class officer, Mr McCulloch, was reputed to have said that he sensed something was going on but could not put his finger on it. Luckily for us, it remained only a slight unease. In 1963 I met Mr McCulloch while on holidays in Bundoran, County Donegal. There was no way to avoid one another. 'Hello, Mr McCulloch,' I greeted him and when asked what I was doing there I replied, 'Like yourself, on holidays.' We had a friendly but stilted conversation before departing.

John and I were now faced with a dilemma. We were behind schedule and needed more time to finish the work. We decided that John should continue cutting that night when we were locked up in our cells, and so after tea and recreation he recommenced. After a few strokes of the blade which I could hear distinctly from my cell above, I gave a pre-agreed knock for him to desist. Then I wrote a note which with a line of thread I lowered down the wall to his cell. A knock told him that there was a 'thread mail' waiting for him at the window and he climbed up and took it in. The note was in Irish and in code. He replied in the same way. We agreed that John should continue cutting sporadically, not allowing time for the source of the noise to be identified. I stood at my door looking out through the peephole and listening intently for any sound of footsteps from John's landing. It was a tense hour or so during which John made good progress.

In the morning, Christmas Eve, the noise level increased accordingly with trolleys moving along the wings and buckets being assembled for the slop out. John took the opportunity to

cut as much of the window frame as he could, as this created
a loud screeching sound. There were no more opportunities
to make headway that day as we would be out of our cells for
breakfast, a walk in the yard and duty in the workshop. One
thing was certain – we would not be making our attempt on
Christmas Eve despite all its benefits, including the fact that
John had arranged to have cars waiting for us outside the prison
to take us towards the Republic as soon as we broke out.

An added fear now was that John's work could be
discovered by an observant officer. We had disguised them well
but a stroke of a baton or a strong tug by hand would have
revealed all. We could do nothing that day but pray. We had to
rethink our timetable. Christmas Day would see us locked up
for twenty hours out of the twenty-four, but there would be
little time for activity as we had Mass and breakfast followed
by two hours recreation in the garden yard before dinner and
lock-up. So we changed our escape date to the following day,
the feast of Stephen.

Christmas Day was when I assembled the rope using my
bed blankets and the electric flex. It was not advisable to start
the rope any earlier as it would have been almost impossible
to conceal. I could not start on the rope until lights out at nine
as the warder checking the cells, sometimes twice an hour,
would observe me very easily. At the appointed time I could
hear him whistling to himself as he switched off every light.
The new security lights on the outside provided enough
illumination for me to see what I was doing. I began to tear
my blankets and sheets into strips. I was hoping the sheets were
made of strong Belfast linen but alas were quite thin, so I only
used the strips of blankets entwined with the electric flex tied
at intervals with strong binder cord. The work was tough as I
entwined each strip of blanket with the electric wire. We had
the added benefit of small pieces of strong cord from the
laundry bags which I used every couple of feet to strengthen
the rope. The regular checking of the cells that night meant
that I was jumping in and out of bed as the warder shone his

torch into the cell and looked through the peephole.

Planning and forecasting are based primarily on experience, but I had no idea how long it would take me to weave a 70-foot rope. In addition, having never stayed up all night before I didn't know how often the security checking took place. I soon realised that I could not do it in one night; all I could manage was a strong rope of about 40 feet with a weak tail of 30 feet. It would have to do. I hid it in my cell in the expectation that there would be no searches on St Stephen's Day, a free day for us prisoners. After breakfast we went for our walk around the yard, from which John's cell was visible. Another republican prisoner had come in to see John about a book, and when he spotted what we were at he retreated very quickly. He said nothing but in the yard I could see him observing John's cell window rather too closely. He was a good friend of mine so was unlikely to go to the unit leader with his suspicions – not that anyone could do much about it except report us to the authorities, and we did not expect that to happen. John and I discussed our next move and the final leg of our plan. We would go immediately after tea at around five o'clock. The bars were cut, the rope was made and the die was certainly cast. There was no going back.

The Leaving of Crumlin

Immediately after tea in the dining hall it was imperative that we could access our cells. To our consternation, however, the officer in charge of the gate out of the hall was not an A Wing regular. The regular warders were more adaptable than those assigned to A Wing on an infrequent basis, who operated as they would in the short-term section where few favours were granted. The warder refused John's request to go to his cell. I was reduced to begging him to let John out 'to get a table tennis ball' and eventually he relented and called the officer on the wing to accompany John. Now I also had to get to the wing. The warder and I were engaged in a discussion about Christmas when I suddenly pretended to realise that we had no table tennis bats either. 'I won't be a minute. I'll be right back,' I ventured. With a shrug of impatience he said, 'OK then' and called Mr Rampf to escort me to my cell. Rampf followed my every footstep and really gave me grief. But as outlined previously we managed to outmanoeuvre him and I made my way to John's cell on A2.

First we had to use brute strength to break off the frame which held the panes of glass as we had neither the time nor the opportunity to complete the final cut. Using the strong wooden handle of a heavy buffer used for polishing the floors we pressed the frame back as if on a hinge. This took about four minutes. We had the assistance of Séamus McRory, who had volunteered to act as lookout and to pass down our jackets when we reached the ground. At this point former O/C Tom Mitchell entered John's cell but immediately retreated when he heard the sound of metal and wood grinding. We were now under pressure and in real danger of being caught before we even got out of the cell. But before long, despite all the near misses and obstacles, we were out in the open. Fate decreed that only I would make it all the way.

Lying there on the ground outside the main prison wall I thought I had broken my back. The pain was excruciating, but after a few attempts I managed to get up. The main problem now was my foot, or more accurately my heel. The pain was piercing. All the time I kept looking up expecting to see John drop, as I was to break his fall. The sleet and snow were swirling around and the security lights on the outside of the wall were distorting the images. Conscious that I was within sight of the gun towers and that I was using up valuable time, I called out for John one last time in a low voice as I thought I saw his form at the edge of the high wall. Standing on my tiptoes I discovered that I could move as long as I did not put any weight on my heel. Taking one last look up I reverted to the emergency plan we agreed in the event that we became separated. Although John had outlined the roads in the area for me, I was now very much on my own.

I was hoping against hope that the outside contacts organised for Christmas Eve would have decided to come to the prison again that evening. They knew something had happened to us two days earlier but we could not get word to them to make other arrangements. Outside the prison I turned left towards the city, following John's map in my head. I was unaware that a police car had just delivered a prisoner from Derry to the main gate or that by now Mr Rampf had alerted his superiors to the possibility that two prisoners had escaped. If John had been with me we would not have taken this route into the city. He would have led us to a less obvious place.

My only option was to find my way to Kellys' house in Adela Street. John's brother Billy had just been released from internment in D Wing and my hope was that he would direct me to a safe place. I knew that once the authorities identified John as my accomplice, his would be the first house raided. So I had to move fast. I ran down Crumlin Road and after the Mater Hospital I noticed a road entrance (Fleetwood Street) which was in darkness and which would have led me to Adela Street. Here I made a wrong decision. I reckoned the turning was merely an entrance to a business yard and so I ran on in the blinding sleet. There was very little traffic on the streets and no pedestrians. I ran all the way down to Carlisle Circus and at the top of Clifton Street turned left into Henry Place. But when I found myself on Glenravel Street, which in those days housed an important RUC station, I knew I had gone too far and was heading further away from my planned destination.

Just as I realised my error I ran past two RUC men standing in a darkened shop doorway. I caught them in my peripheral vision and as I looked back I saw that they had come out of the doorway and were looking after me as I ran. I kept running, despite knowing that I had to go back up past them again on my way to Adela Street. A reasonable distance away a bus was coming towards me on the other side. I ran diagonally across the road as if taking the next junction and just when I thought I was invisible to the two policemen I turned quickly and kept running on the blind side of the bus back past them. Success! As the bus accelerated I took time to step into a concealed doorway to establish if the two policemen had worked it out yet. To my relief they were both still looking down Glenravel Street in the opposite direction to where I was. Their lack of action told me that the alarm had not yet been sounded.

By now I was slightly disorientated. I spotted two people walking and ran towards them for directions but when they saw me they took off. This concerned me as I knew my appearance was now a hindrance to my escape. I was dressed in shirt, grey trousers, socks and canvas slippers. I was also covered in muck from crawling along the walls, my shirt was soaking and my face spattered with dirt. Nevertheless, I had better luck with three other pedestrians. I asked if I was on the right road for the Mater Hospital, explaining that I had been in a car crash and needed help. They confirmed my direction. I learned later that they were unionists and had gone immediately to the police when the alarm went off. Back on Crumlin Road I ran to the dark entrance (Fleetwood Street) and spotted a young woman standing at the bus stop near the junction. Unlike my earlier experience, she was smiling widely at me, which gave me the confidence to ask, 'Will this lead me to Adela Street?' She was so effusive that I thought she would have come with me if I had asked her. I imagined her to be a Catholic nurse who was coming off duty in the Mater Hospital. Mrs Kelly subsequently confirmed that I was correct. There was no time to lose. Finding myself in Adela Street, I looked for number 12 and knocked on the door.

Belfast Town and the Kelly Family

A young boy opened the door. As soon as I saw his face I knew I was at the right house. He was Oliver, fourteen years old. When I asked, 'Is your Mammy or Daddy in?' he immediately opened the kitchen door and said, 'Come on in.' It was such a welcome – and such a relief. He acted as though escaping prisoners knocked on his door every day. His mother and father were in the kitchen preparing the evening meal when I entered. I told them my name and that I had escaped from the prison and that John might be along after me if he was not injured. As I stood there looking less than presentable, Mrs Kelly turned to her husband and with a great smile said, 'Ah, William, look at him and his rosary beads around his neck. Sure God bless him.' Otherwise she made no comment about my appearance except to say, in an urgent voice but one that betrayed no panic, 'Take those slippers off you immediately, the dogs will be here within twenty minutes.' She exuded a sense of authority and wisdom based on hard experience and I did as I was told. She immediately took the slippers and stuffed them into the burning flames of the Stanley range.

As John's parents discussed my options, a feeling of sheer confidence almost overwhelmed me. In prison we pored over all potential obstacles once outside, but I cannot remember any talk of destroying our footwear to frustrate the police dogs. I felt that if anyone in Belfast could direct me towards freedom in the Republic, it was the Kellys. Within a minute or so they agreed on one particular house that had no connection with the republican movement.

The Kellys were highly respected within their own neighbourhood, by churchmen in Belfast and among the business community with whom they worked on a daily basis. Internees and released sentenced prisoners had a standing invitation to go directly to their house where they would receive a great welcome, a meal, good advice, directions or lifts to bus and train stations and, on many occasions, money. The Kelly household was revered in republican circles not only throughout the North but among many in the South also. They gave me a pair of wellington boots and an overcoat and Mr Kelly and Oliver walked with me at a quick pace towards a house not too far away and still quite near the prison. Mr Kelly knocked on the door, quickly briefed the woman who answered and said he would be back for me in the morning. The woman, in her early forties, gave me a warm welcome.

Mrs Margaret Kelly's grandfather was a great friend of James Connolly when he lived in Belfast. Her uncle Billy Maginness was his election agent when Connolly stood for election. As a young girl Mrs Kelly accompanied Winfred Carney, Connolly's secretary, everywhere on political errands throughout the city so from an early age was imbued with the struggle for civil rights, workers' rights and the independence of Ireland. Margaret and William's younger children, Jimmy, Oliver and Rita, prepared vegetable parcels for internees every Saturday which included salads, beetroot, tomatoes and every kind of vegetable and fruit available in those days. It must have cost them a sizeable portion of their profit margin. In later years Rita set up the Irish Caucus in Washington with Fr Seán McManus, which had a seminal influence during the thirty years' war. It is said by well-informed commentators that their contribution was the primary factor in engaging both the Democratic and Republican Parties in the northern situation. Rita passed away in November 2009. Two of her brothers, Billy and Oliver, both well known for their republican credentials and commitment to justice, died the year before. Oliver qualified as a solicitor while interned in Crumlin Road during the 1970s and went on to become a leading defence lawyer. He became a mentor for Pat Finucane, who was later assassinated in 1989. Oliver's name was also on the assassination list. The Kellys were intertwined with the GAA in Belfast and Oliver was at one time chairman of the County Board, a position he held for ten years.

John himself had a extraordinary life when the Civil Rights campaign unnerved the unionists in 1969. He led the defence of his community against the loyalist squads who burned down Catholic houses and churches, and involved the Irish government in the importation of arms to protect his people. Following the 1994 and 1998 ceasefires John returned north and was elected a Member of the Legislative Assembly

(MLA) for South Derry. He died aged seventy-two in September 2007.

John's mother, Mrs Kelly, was herself shot by loyalists who attacked a Hunger Strike protest group in Belfast in October 1980. Her son Billy was in a mock-up cage cell covered in a blanket in a stationary protest on the New Lodge Road and she called over to greet him as she returned from evening Mass in St Patrick's Church. Just at that moment a passing car unleashed a hail of bullets, five of which hit Mrs Kelly in the back. Amazingly she survived, but one bullet could not be extracted and she lived with it in her body for another two years before she died in 1983. My story goes back twenty-three years before that and underlines the sacrifices that some people made to create a better, safer and more just Ireland. The entire Kelly family exuded concern and support for the underdog, no matter what that person's religion or politics. In line with their unchallengeable republican credentials, they were scrupulously non-sectarian and, indeed, could be described as anti-sectarian. I was fortunate to know them and feel proud to have been associated with them.

In the safe house there was a welcoming fire and the table had been set for the woman of the house and her family. I kept my boots and overcoat on and sat in an armchair in front of the fire. There were children playing with their Christmas toys and, of course, showing them to me. The woman gave me tea and bread and as I sat there I was aware of the severe pain in my hand and leg. Unknown to me then, I had broken a bone in both my hand and heel and had also hurt my back. The woman gave me an aspirin to dull the pain – exactly what Dr McComb would have recommended! She told me she had seven children, all living at home and indeed all there that evening. The fire and the tea made me feel much easier as we discussed what kind of searches would take place following my escape. It was all so perfectly normal that it was almost surreal. As we sat there the prison siren started to wail. It was so loud it could have been outside her living-room window.

Flares lit up the sky from the new RUC headquarters on Ladas Drive; it the first time they were used and seemingly frightened the life out of residents living nearby. The BBC and UTV news gave details of the breakout and showed the photograph of me taken when I was fingerprinted in 1957. The same picture was carried by all the newspapers in the following days.

The woman said she expected all the houses in her road to be searched that night by police and dogs. In such circumstances I could stay there no longer. I understood her predicament and had full sympathy with her. As well as that, I did not want to be a sitting duck. When I asked where I could go her young son spoke up and said when he played hide-and-seek he often climbed on to the roof of a large open-sided transport shed near where they lived. The shed belonged to a prominent unionist family, the Morgans. James Morgan was at the time Assistant Parliamentary Secretary to the Ministry of Finance in Stormont. I considered this a good option, so she and her son and daughter took me out the back and up a lane behind the houses to the back of the transport depot. The boy explained that I would see a trapdoor in the centre of the roof that led down to the shed. If I was lucky, he told me, there would be a lorry parked immediately under the trapdoor. On occasions the driver did not lock the doors and if that was so I could sit in the cab of the lorry out of the bitter cold.

Another bloody wall, I thought. It was not as high as the prison wall but as I climbed, the pain in my leg and hand was almost unbearable. Fortunately, the wall was full of indents which facilitated my climb. As I crawled towards the trapdoor, searchlights flashed across the roof as if picking me out. I remained perfectly still until I realised that the lights were merely the extended beams from the searchlights from the prison walls. On opening the trapdoor, to my great satisfaction I saw the steel roof of a large lorry parked directly underneath. There was a drop of about 5 feet which was a challenge because my body by this time was wracked with pain. Getting on the roof of the lorry was a small victory for me and I was now able to close the trapdoor. While it was an open shed I was, at least, protected from the sleet. My next objective was to see if I could descend the cab of the lorry and establish if the door was open. It was so bitterly cold that the imagined warmth of the cab was a real incentive for a Herculean effort on my part to climb down and get in. However, having left the heat of the living room my body temperature had dropped significantly in a short space of time and a creeping stiffness in every limb left me much less supple and mentally unable to risk another fall if I lost my step in the dark. My only option was to lie on top and keep myself warm with my own breath.

Pulling the collar of my overcoat over my mouth and tucking my head into my coat I tried to warm myself by breathing in the enclosed space. It brought some comfort for a time. There was a public clock in the vicinity which pealed out the time every quarter of an hour. I heard seven o'clock. After a little while I could see a lot of activity on the main Antrim Road just opposite where I was. It was an RUC roadblock. Every car was stopped and then waved on by the red police light. Having the police in such close proximity was rather nerve-wracking as I thought it might be a prelude to a search of yards and sheds like the one I was in. As evening turned into night the roadblock was ended and I thought I noticed the outline of two peaked police caps in the shed. I lay motionless, fearing even to breathe. I kept my eye on them and was amazed that they could match me for patience and stillness. Because I lay so still my body really stiffened up as I desisted from the leg- and arm-moving exercises that had kept me both mobile and warm. After several hours, however, I realised that it was merely a trick of the light. The two 'peaked caps' were in fact the slanted edges of the eaves.

Time moved on and the voices from the houses nearby resounded with laughter and on occasion music and song as residents held their St Stephen's Day parties. This made me feel lonesome and my thoughts turned to the plight of John

Kelly. Had he got away? Had he been caught? Was he mistreated? As it was Christmas holiday time I did not expect to hear many people or traffic circulating early – nor did I. Every so often I would slide the trapdoor back to peek out to establish if there was any movement in the general vicinity. Apart from the police vehicles and the sporadic barking of their dogs, everything became generally quiet.

I learned later that John Kelly had been placed in solitary confinement and subjected to a charge of attempting to escape and of assisting me. Solitary confinement meant no company except prison officers and reduced rations of food and for the first days only bread and water. He also lost all privileges such as receiving letters or tobacco. He was confined to his cell during the hours of association in the evening for six months. Part of the automatic remission for good behaviour was forfeited, resulting in an additional six months in prison. Later, however, he told me that, although the authorities were obviously outraged by his attempted escape, he was not ill-treated in a brutal manner. In fact one of the Belfast-born warders, not known for his friendliness to republicans, would surreptitiously throw him two cigarettes bound together with a match as he banged the cell door closed. He had also to contend with the ire of some of the IRA leadership in A Wing on his return. A number of them attempted to have John isolated but they failed, as most of the political prisoners were delighted with the escape. The gripe was that they should have been told in advance so that they would be prepared for the searches. But perhaps the real reason for the discontent of the few was that they always preached that an escape was impossible and we shattered that myth.

I knew I had to leave my den before daylight, if possible around 8 a.m. I had to avoid being seen as I crawled back across the corrugated roof. I pushed aside the trapdoor, hauled myself up on to the roof and gingerly crawled to the edge beside the laneway. I could not believe that the searchlights were still active and I lay still three or four times before I reached the edge. I had to steel myself for the drop down as there was no doubt that I was in poor physical shape as a result of hypothermia and injury. However, my youth and fitness programme equipped me well for the challenge. Back on the ground I retraced my steps of the previous night. But immediately I was seized by an unexpected dilemma. All the back doors to the terraced houses seemed identical, apart from colour. But of course the previous night it was dark and I was not aware of the colours. I concentrated hard. Based on instinct and a good sense of direction I decided on a particular door. I entered the back yard and when I tried the door of the house it opened. But unlocked back doors were the norm in those years so I took little consolation from this. I went into the kitchen and then the living room but there was nothing I could recognise. The blazing fire was dead. The table set for tea was bare and covered with an embroidered cloth. The armchair was in a different position and looked nothing like the one I sat in. I went back out to the kitchen and looked in a little mirror above the sink. I was startled to see the haggard, worn-out look on my face. I could run no more so went back into the living room and sat on a high chair near the door.

Thinking about how I would handle the situation if I was in the wrong house I thought I had better get it over with before it was too late. With a sweeping brush I knocked hard on the ceiling but despite doing this several times no one came down. After about two hours I heard footsteps on the stairs. I had thought out my plan of action if the person was hostile but when the door opened I was filled with a sense of relief. 'Ah, you managed to get back,' said the woman of the house. However, she followed this with 'You know you cannot stay here tonight.' As the police had not raided her house already they would surely do so that night. But at least I would have a number of hours to prepare my exit out of Belfast.

I had given much thought during the night to how I would avoid the roadblocks and establish a route out of the city. While Belfast was, at that time, a unionist city with an atmosphere of dominance over the minority nationalist population, I knew from my days in prison that there was a great underbelly of resentment against the authorities that could only be described as fearless. If I could tap into this, my efforts to thwart the powers that be would be well supported. This knowledge and understanding played a vital role in my arriving at various possible scenarios and allowed me to overcome the sense of inevitable failure that had marked many of the IRA actions over recent years.

Sitting down to breakfast I had time to consider in detail all the options open to me. We agreed that I would leave around five o'clock. The woman of the house became a kind of co-conspirator. As the children came down for breakfast, she and her eldest daughter decided they would have to keep them inside all day as one of them might have let slip that there was a strange man in their house. This was another reflection of how the ordinary nationalist people seemed to have an in-built protection system at work.

The woman's husband was working in England. Many Catholic men at this time were forced to emigrate to find work and many lived in sad, dilapidated conditions in England, sending home most of their hard-earned money to feed their family. They missed birthdays, anniversaries and sometimes even Christmas. I had missed my three nephews when I was in prison but here was a man who could not even enjoy the happiness of his own seven children at Christmas time. He and his wife have now gone to their eternal reward.

When I had parted company with Mr Kelly and Oliver there was an expectation that we would be in contact some time the following day. But I feared that such a meeting would be impossible given the levels of security. However, there was a need to find out if the Kelly family had any suggestions and so the woman of the house sent her daughter to ask a trusted neighbour to come to the house. She was flabbergasted when she saw me and told me there were police and soldiers everywhere. I gave her instructions to go on an errand which would bring her near or past Kellys' house. She returned to say that Kellys' was like an army camp with hundreds of police in battledress. The house was surrounded and no one but police could go in or out. The latest information on the street was that the Kelly family had all been arrested. The eldest daughter, Margaret, and her husband, who had just returned from Canada, had gone to Dublin by car for the day with her brother Billy and his girlfriend and a friend. On returning they were all arrested as there was an erroneous assumption by the RUC that they had whisked me across the border. Another brother, Jimmy, and a pal had also crossed the border, quite separately from the others, and were arrested in Dundalk by Gardaí and handed over to the RUC.

Several options were examined and one or two tested theoretically before being dropped. One was to establish if there was a funeral anywhere nearby that I could join. I knew that if I could somehow manage to get in among a group of Belfast Catholic men there was a good chance of someone arranging a car to drive me towards the border in south Armagh. As there were no morning papers, we were deprived of the obituary lists. So our neighbour went off again to acquire information. The news was not good; there was nothing anywhere near. We would have to think again.

11

THE GREEN PIMPERNEL

I decided to head for Dungannon via Cookstown. The relatively small population of active republicans in Belfast would be watched with an eagle eye by the RUC Special Branch and so I could not expect any assistance from people who would have been only too willing to help. There were several people in Dungannon whom I knew both from Sinn Féin politics and from football matches. I felt this would be the best route towards the border. But of course there were a few obstacles. I was still dressed in my prison clothes and my leg was very stiff. I asked the woman if I could borrow some of her husband's clothes. When I looked in the wardrobe I couldn't believe what I found. Among some coats and trousers was a Civil Defence uniform with the words 'Her Majesty's Civil Defence' embroidered in gold on the shoulders. I tried it on and it fitted perfectly. It came complete with a heavy overcoat and a beret, all bearing the words. I added a white shirt and matching tie and a pair of the man's shoes and walked back downstairs. 'Oh, you can't wear that, my husband would kill me if I lost that uniform,' the woman protested. She was rightly concerned that if I was captured they could trace the uniform. I convinced her that I would successfully escape and that the uniform would be back in her wardrobe within a week. We also agreed that if I was captured she was to go immediately to the nearest police station and report the uniform missing. For my part I would not answer any questions but would admit that I burgled a house and stole the clothes. Several days later, before I had even crossed the border, the uniform was back in the wardrobe.

The neighbour went on her last errand for me that day. She went back to her own house and fetched several pairs of old spectacles, one of which I wore as a final part of my disguise. The woman of the house gave me the price of the bus fare and some additional money out of her scarce resources. I promised to return both the money and the spectacles; I kept my word. The bus left for Cookstown at six from the Antrim Road. One of the daughters escorted me as she knew the way. The streets were covered in ice, making it hard to walk. I instructed the young girl to walk ahead of me slowly enough for me to keep up, and never to look back in case anyone was watching. When she came to the bus stop she was to stop and look in at the nearest shop window. That would be her signal that I was at the right stop. She was very natural and calm. We parted, as planned, without any acknowledgement to each other and I took up my position at the bus stop. Unfortunately I was the only person standing there. Even more unfortunately I was the only one standing on the street that bitterly cold night. An unmarked car with what looked like four or five Special Branch detectives drove up right beside me, staring at me. I remained calm. My concern was that one of them may have been part of the convoy at the hospital earlier that month. After what seemed an eternity they drove off at high speed. Just then a lady came half walking, half running, loaded with parcels asking me was she at the right bus stop for Cookstown. I was delighted to have a companion and immediately confirmed that it was and that it should arrive soon. We spoke of the hard winter and dreadful sleet and snow and now the hard frost.

The bus arrived and I helped the woman on with her parcels, hoping to sit with her and engage her in conversation to create an impression that we were together. All my work was for nothing, however, as she selected a seat beside another passenger. I made my way down the fairly packed bus and sat in a seat in the middle. Unknown to me this bus also served the suburbs of Belfast. As I sat trying to appear inconspicuous, the passenger in the seat in front opened his *Belfast Telegraph* with the heading 'Donnelly still on the run'. The top of the paper was taken up with a large photograph of me across two columns. It was the image of a man you would not want to meet on a dark night. I prayed that he would turn to some other news, but no, he wanted to read all about it. He kept the paper high above his head as he read the small print. I looked out the window and also read a copy of an old paper I had taken with me as a distraction. Just then the driver braked hard and brought the bus to a stop. The regular passengers seemed puzzled and within seconds four policemen boarded and walked down the middle aisle looking at everyone, including me. Again I avoided eye contact as I was engrossed in my newspaper. They left empty-handed.

The journey took us around the east and north side of Lough Neagh before turning down the west side towards my destination. Going through Toomebridge, my heart leapt with the tune of 'Roddy McCorley' in my head. We had grown up with that rebel song about the terrible death meted out to a young Presbyterian who had fought against the British in 1798 and paid for his radicalism a year later on the bridge of Toome. And here I was crossing that bridge being hunted by the same British. The memory gave me added strength.

I had now left Antrim and was in County Derry. The journey northwards away from the border was quite fortuitous and could be considered an added bonus in terms of searches and roadblocks. The police expected me to head for the border and probably considered it unlikely that I would head further north. Having passed Castledawson and Magherafelt I was taken by surprise when we reached Moneymore in County Derry on the west side of Lough Neagh.

As passengers alighted the remaining nine or ten,

including myself, were instructed to change buses for Cookstown. I was not happy about being in a bus with so few passengers as I now stood out in my uniform which was an unusual one for the country areas. Despite looking around to find a travelling companion as a distraction, they were all locals who were together and had no interest in a stranger. Moneymore was a name I was familiar with as my parents had good friends in Derry, both city and county. The town was known to me as a unionist stronghold and so the sooner I was gone from it the better. As the bus navigated the little streets, we eventually took the Cookstown road.

Surrounded by Police

Just as I was settling down for the remainder of the journey, I was rudely aroused by the sudden stopping of the bus not far outside Moneymore. The windows were covered in condensation and when I cleared the window with my hand I noticed a massive roadblock with police and plainclothes Special Branch men supported by B Specials in uniform. The uniformed police got on board and began to question each of the ten passengers individually. As I was seated near the front of the bus they were nearly all questioned before me. My heart sank as I heard the police say as they came to each of the other passengers, 'Hello Sammy, Hello Willie, Hello Malcolm . . .' and other Christian names usually associated with Protestants at that time.

After what seemed an eternity a policeman arrived at my seat. 'Good evening, sir, what is your name and where are you going and where are you coming from?' I looked him in the eye through the old lady's spectacles and said that I was John Walsh coming from Belfast on my way to Dungannon. He then asked me my business there and I explained that I had been called out to substitute for another colleague to carry out year-end stocktaking in the Dungannon depot. He looked at my uniform and it was obvious to me that he was unfamiliar with the Civil Defence and asked, 'What section of the forces do you belong to?' With as much authority and loyalty as I could manage I replied out loud, 'Her Majesty's Civil Defence Force.' He then asked me to furnish him with some paper identification. I explained that as I had left Belfast in a hurry owing to the emergency request and had not stopped to bring anything of that nature with me. Rather reluctantly, he left me and the bus. After a few seconds two plainclothes Special Branch men came to the window where I was sitting and stared in at me through the clearing I had made earlier with my hand. The photograph I had seen in the *Telegraph* earlier that evening was taken four years previously and, in my opinion, would not identify me at a quick glance. However, I was aware that the police look out for jaw structure, shape of the mouth and eyes and often, despite very good disguises, they can successfully identify their quarry. This is exactly what they were doing now and I had unthinkingly given them the opportunity by cleaning the window. They stopped looking at me but the bus did not move. To my discomfort, if not distress, the same policeman came back to me and said, 'You must have some identification on your person.' Again I explained that I hadn't and even pulled out the lining of two of my pockets to show him that they were empty. He left again and having obviously had another discussion with his superiors outside came back to me a third time asking me in a very serious tone of voice was I sure I had no identification papers. On this occasion I used the name of the head of the Civil Defence in Belfast which I had asked the lady for in case of such an event. I mentioned his name as if he was a nationally known figure and suggested that he could contact him to verify my errand. He said that was not really satisfactory and he reluctantly left me while he conferred again outside. I waited with bated breath for him to return and ask me to leave the bus and go to the RUC station in Moneymore. I was now busy contemplating my options, which were rather restricted due to my physical condition. Would I run or would I try and bluff it out for another while until a better opportunity arose?

I said a few prayers to my patron, St Joseph. To my astonishment and relief the bus pulled away, and as it did so I could feel the eyes of the other passengers on me.

On the journey to Cookstown, just fifteen miles from Moneymore, my mind was in turmoil. Had they recognised me and were they now trailing me to see what contacts I would make? At one stage I was convinced this was the case and planned accordingly. I reached Cookstown and established that there was a bus to Dungannon later that night but, because of frost on the roads, the time was not certain. During the Second World War American soldiers were stationed outside Cookstown and it also had an internment camp for captured German soldiers. Because of this I associated it with the authorities and was not keen to spend too much time there. My plan was to disappear in case the police were following me. The hiding place I chose was the local cinema. I checked the price, which I could just afford, and waited around so that if I was being watched my 'trail' would have either gone to report back or to park the car. After a few minutes I asked the cashier if there was a clock in the cinema. There was not. I explained that as I had to catch a bus later I could not go in since I had no watch. The cashier was very pleasant but had no solution so I went out on to the street again. In a fish and chip shop I ordered a plate of chips. I took off my beret to eat – reluctantly, as I was now more easily identifiable. My mother told me later that I should have kept it on as Protestant men did not always bare their heads when eating.

I asked where to get the bus for Dungannon and was directed to a stop in a busy area with the added information that if I went to the UTA (Ulster Transport Association) garage I could board the bus there. The garage was off the main street and there was not much public lighting around, which suited me. Seated beside a large brazier in the garage were two men, one of whom was the driver of the Dungannon bus. It was a cosy place and I was happy to sit down and share the heat.

Another man arrived and we chatted about the weather. I was anxious to discover 'what side of the house' they were from but all three were very cagey. From their Christian names I took the view that they were Protestants. Word came that the Dungannon bus would be very late due to the conditions. This was bad news as I wanted to reach Dungannon before people went to bed. No one was expecting me there and I was not sure where I would seek help. What I did know, though, was that there were plenty who would be only too happy to assist.

Suddenly the driver asked, 'What branch of the forces do you belong to and what do you do?' Fortunately I had read several weeks earlier in the *Reader's Digest* an article about Civil Defence activity in Sweden and proceeded to give them a master class on the subject until the bus arrived. I was happy to have brought a new dimension to their fireside chats! On the bus I sat beside one of the three, Willie, who after a while decided I was one of 'his' and in a whisper advised me to be very careful in Dungannon as it was a 'black hole', a 'Fenian' town.

I recognised several faces as they boarded and alighted along the way. I knew them from Gaelic football matches I had attended in earlier years and it was reassuring to know I was among my own again. Eventually we arrived in the main square in Dungannon. The footpaths were treacherous with ice, which actually helped me disguise my limp. I knew the police would assume I had injured myself when jumping and indeed I learned later that the public had been alerted that the escapee might well walk with a limp. I slowly picked my steps to avoid falling and to disguise my injury, which was becoming more painful and perhaps more obvious. The streets were quiet except for a group of police and B Specials in the town square. I walked past them but did not engage in conversation.

I knew of one particular republican family in the centre of the town. If they could not help, I was sure they could direct me to a safe house. Waiting until there was no one around, I knocked on the door. The place was in darkness and no one answered, even after a second loud knock. I had to move on. My next move was a real risk but it was late and freezing and I needed shelter and hopefully good connections. One of our Dungannon footballer friends was friendly with a girl whose house was not far away. We had been with them a couple of times and I remembered the house. Her father, however, was a businessman and would have no experience of dealing with someone like me. But my options were few so I walked from one street to another and eventually reached the house. The girl herself answered. She did not recognise me in my disguise but neither did she show any concern about such a late caller. Immediately I asked if I could speak to her father, whom I had never met. When he appeared I stood back slightly and said in a low voice, 'Hello, Mr —, I am Danny Donnelly. Could you direct me to Charlemont Street?' His demeanour exuded support. He shook my hand and wished me well and gave me excellent directions. He also gave me his word that he would tell no one I was in Dungannon.

The Moneymore roadblock was still bothering me and as I limped along I took frequent opportunities to keep an eye out on all sides. When certain that I was not being followed I made progress towards Charlemont Street. On approaching the house I spotted a young fellow with identical features to my friend Paddy Devlin. He told me that Paddy lived in the house but that only Teddy was there at that time. Teddy and Paddy were interned in D Wing and had been released just a short time before. The young lad ran down the street and entered the house while I took refuge in the shadows. Like Kellys in Belfast, it was not a safe house as everyone knew their republican politics.

Teddy Devlin came out and I told him that I needed help. He invited me into the house. Sitting in the large living room by a roaring fire were his parents. They gave me a great welcome. Immediately they sent for other family members who came in within seconds. They lived just next door and across the street. Teddy's grandparents were there also. They extended their hospitality and prepared a meal, during which I told them of my escape so far and the Moneymore road-block and that I had taken a man in Dungannon into my confidence despite not knowing him.

My hand and foot were bandaged and I was given tablets to ease the pain. The eldest boy, John, and his wife, Betty, invited me to stay in their house across the road. The thinking was that if any house was to be raided it would be the home place. From across the road such activity would be quickly spotted and I could leave via the back lane. The warmth of their welcome and the medical treatment gave me new life. That night I slept in a luxurious double bed. I fell asleep and was conscious of dreaming or perhaps hallucinating. I could see the sleety sky as I relived the previous night pulling back the trapdoor and looking out from my cold hiding place. I awoke in the morning light to find a priest dressed in full collar and black suit looking down on me.

An Sagart a Rún

He was like a vision but his presence brought a semblance of normality to my situation.

He exuded confidence and charm and he had charisma. He congratulated me on the escape and talked about the numerous roadblocks set up all around the county. I did not know him. He made a reference to the escape of Red Hugh O'Donnell at Christmas time in 1592 and was amused when I told him that it was no coincidence. He impressed me with his ability to make the connection so swiftly and after he left I was told that his name was an t-Athair Éamonn Ó Doibhlin and that he was a noted historian among many other talents. He would later officiate at my wedding in 1967; he died in 1972 aged sixty-two. He gave me his blessing as I lay there in the bed, promised that he would call again and left to carry out his other duties.

How life changes so quickly. While I lay there resting, my

hosts and I discussed the uniform and the need for it to be returned post-haste. The danger was that if the Cookstown roadblock police realised that the man they questioned was me, the authorities might recall all such uniforms in an effort to identify the owner of mine. This was a real concern as when questioned I had asserted that I was going to the Civil Defence store in Dungannon to take end of year stock. To my anxiety I learned that there was no such store in Dungannon. The very next day both the uniform and borrowed money were delivered back to the woman in Belfast. In the meantime John had provided me with civilian clothes and I got dressed.

I had serious concerns about landing myself on these good people and made up my mind that my stay would be as short as possible. The family member I knew was out of town and my plans were based around him. He was not aware of my escape and in his absence the responsibility fell to his other family members, who were magnificent. It was too risky to go back to Omagh, so another option was to make contact with people in east and south Tyrone whom I felt could bring me safely across the border. At that time there was no extradition treaty between the UK and the Republic of Ireland; such a treaty only became law in 1978. So as soon as I was in the Republic I was free.

I decided to make contact with another former internee called Paddy Joe McClean, who lived between Ballgawley and Beragh. That area had a myriad of narrow roads leading to the Mass Rock in Altamuskin, the mountains of Pomeroy, Carrickmore, Aughnacloy and – most important of all at that moment – Emyvale in County Monaghan. It was agreed that I should not stay longer than one night in Devlins but should move to another house that night. The priest returned that evening and his plan was simple, although not entirely to my liking. He would reverse his Morris Minor car up to the back door of the house in Charlemont Street and open the boot, into which I would go. He would then drive through the roadblocks to his home in a neighbouring village. I was stiff and sore and getting into the boot of a Morris Minor is a chore at the best of times. I felt very vulnerable, not being in control of my own destiny. But he was certain it would work and I conceded to his plan. He was not stopped on the journey but told me later that there were plenty of police. At the parochial house we carried out the same manoeuvre in reverse. The car was parked near the back door and I alighted. His housekeeper was a very homely woman who met me at the door with a great welcome.

After some small talk she showed me to the guest room. Once again I had a double bed and she even placed a glass of milk on the side locker. I slept soundly, thinking how lucky I was to be in such a place with so much support. The priest had a busy schedule and to minimise suspicion he needed to go about his business in the normal way. He arranged with another family to house me during daylight hours so after breakfast we headed there. Again I was made most welcome by an elderly lady and her adult daughter. Lovely food was served and we sat before another great roaring fire. The daughter, another nurse home on Christmas holidays, very kindly re-bandaged my foot and hand and gave me medicine to dull the pain. I was fortunate to have met not one but two nurses in those painful days. A friend of the family called around and later, after our evening meal, building contractor Plunkett O'Donnell and John Devlin arrived with a pick-up truck to take me back to the priest's house, where he had assembled a number of business people in the sitting room. I was introduced to them one by one and they were all very supportive. The fact that so many people were prepared to risk their business, their reputation and maybe even their freedom for a convicted IRA man demonstrates the extent of the dissatisfaction among Catholics and nationalists with the Stormont government.

Their plan was that I should dress as a golfer and that all of us would drive in a couple of cars across the border to a golf club. It seemed like a practical idea and may well have worked.

I wanted to stick to my own plan to contact P. J. McClean, however. My main objection to their idea, I told them, was the risk that one of them could be arrested if I was caught, which would have been an awful burden for me. There was also the serious concern that the Catholic Church would have been vilified if I was captured in the company of a priest. While some among them were disappointed, I got the sense that others were quite relieved. I was very grateful to them. I never met any of them again but often think of their great courage.

Paddy Devlin had reappeared on the scene and with another good friend made contact with Paddy Joe McClean, who suggested that I make my way to his home the following day. It was decided that I should travel in daylight rather than at night, as traffic levels had begun to increase after the holidays and the stopping and searching of vehicles would be more random. Plunkett O'Donnell once again transported me in his pick-up truck, accompanied also by John Devlin. Our story, if stopped, was that we were on our way to a building site near Ballygawley. We rehearsed our lines and my fictitious name of Joe Coyle. In those vans there was a long drawer at the rear of the vehicle which was used to carry tools and lintels for doors and windows. It was suggested that I hide there, but on further consideration we luckily decided against this and I sat in front with the others. There was a support car ahead to alert us to any police activity on the road.

Paddy and a friend had driven to Paddy Joe McClean's home in Altamuskin to bring him my request. Paddy Joe had just been released some weeks previously from Crumlin Road. He lived at home with his parents and seven siblings. It is important to state that Paddy Joe was not a member of the IRA and had never been a member despite being arrested and interned. On being told of my desire to be brought across the border, Paddy Joe turned to his father, Frank. 'What do you think, Dad?' 'We'll help him,' came the reply. Paddy Joe told me later that the decision was down to his father. Paddy Joe showed great respect for his parents in that instance and I admired him for it. After all, it was their house, not his. The visitors returned to Dungannon while Paddy Joe and his father contacted trusted neighbours.

12

BREAK FOR THE BORDER

Another Unnerving Encounter

As we travelled we kept a watch out for our 'sentry' car. If we saw it coming towards us it meant there was a significant roadblock. The road we were on was good and we were doing a nice speed as we neared our turn-off for Altamuskin. Around a bend we saw to our horror a very large contingent of RUC commandos and B Specials. Commando units were formed to combat the IRA, particularly in border areas. They had a free run of police districts and had an unpleasant reputation. With great skill and without apparent panic Plunkett steered the van in a nice U-turn. We reckoned we were far enough away from the roadblock for them not to have noticed. I suggested that if there was a shop in the area we should go there immediately in case we had been spotted. Plunkett knew of a shop up a lane, turned up accordingly and went in to buy cigarettes. We were out of sight of the main road but unsure what to do next. If we went to the roadblock we would be stopped and questioned. If we went left for Dungannon and they followed us we would have to have an excuse for going back. We decided to head back to Dungannon with the story that we had forgotten a piece of material.

Driving down the lane we saw that the entrance back on

to the main road was blocked by a police tender surrounded by more than a dozen officers. Their guns were cocked, ready to fire and a senior policeman shouted 'Halt!' Plunkett can see his face to this day. 'Why did you turn when you saw the roadblock?' he demanded. 'Very simple,' replied Plunkett, 'I needed to buy cigarettes.' 'Where are they?' asked the RUC man. I picked up the packet from the dashboard. 'Here they are.' To the usual questions of 'where are you going' and 'where are you coming from', Plunkett was able to answer confidently, while John and I remained quiet. Then we were asked our names and where we came from. We answered them civilly. The tension was high and I could feel the control slipping away from us as they walked around the van, staring at us. I was dreading the demand to get out as that would mean going to the local RUC station, possibly for fingerprinting. Our fears were fuelled when the senior man demanded that Plunkett get out and open the drawer in the base of the van.

At this point I was now on the side where most of the police had congregated and decided to distract them by opening the cigarette packet. I took one for myself before offering one to John and the nearest policeman. The officer accepted it and we discussed the weather during the previous days and how it affected traffic and so on. John and I blew a lot of smoke around the cab. It was the best we could do. Plunkett had not convinced this senior man that he was an innocent abroad. Having been interned in Crumlin Road during the 1940s, he was a well-known republican. He was asked for his driving licence and insurance, both of which were back in his house. The RUC man was not impressed, and debated out loud whether he should bring us back to the station while Plunkett retrieved his licence and insurance. The only positive aspect was that the attention was firmly focused on poor Plunkett rather than me. Eventually, with very severe instructions to bring his licence and insurance to Dungannon RUC station that evening, Plunkett was allowed to drive on. It was a terrifying ordeal. Our hearts were beating as never before. As the logic for going back to Dungannon had now been superseded, we decided to head for our original destination.

In the meantime we had lost sight of the support car, but met up with it in Ballygawley with some additional local support. After a hasty conversation we continued towards Altamuskin. At Paddy Joe's I bade farewell to John and Plunkett and also thanked profusely Paddy Devlin and the other occupants of the support car. Paddy Joe was on the roadside and immediately brought me into the house. I will never forget the scene. His parents, Minnie and Frank, had the children all lined up in the kitchen. I shook hands with them all as I limped from one to the other.

Altamuskin and the Break for the Border

Paddy Joe led me out through the back door and up a hill to a barn situated between two sand hills. He and his father had organised neighbours to assist in covering my tracks and watching out for police or B Special activity. It was early afternoon and still bright. It was also cold and showery. There was a panoramic view of the whole area from the barn, which was warm from the hay brought in to feed the cattle. From here we could see any search activity that might be in operation, and so lay on the stacks of hay looking out across the countryside. I related my story to Paddy Joe and we also discussed his years in D Wing. The plan was that we would stay in an empty house that night belonging to neighbours. It stood on a hill only accessible by car through a narrow lane. It had a vantage point from the back bedroom window in that there was clear sight of the other side of the hill and the connecting roads. Car lights could be seen from a distance and there were three potential escape routes. The kind neighbours found legitimate reasons to be out on the road late at night as an extra cordon of security while I slept. There were three of us in the house, which was lit by a paraffin lamp. The curtains were closed tightly and food was brought by the owner. The following evening we were going to break for the border. Driving across was a real risk without any options if we were stopped, so our plan was to walk across country, through the fields and bog land.

After Paddy Joe and I left the house to climb the hill to the hay barn, Frank had gone outside to casually brush the street, giving an impression of normality while also keeping an eye out for anything suspicious. We had not left the back yard when an unmarked police car came to a screeching halt outside the door. Without getting out of the car the driver interrogated Frank about the whereabouts of a blue van they had seen near the house. Frank, conscious of how close they were and how unexpected their presence was, very calmly and courteously directed them in precisely the wrong direction. I owe my freedom to many people's bravery and Frank's coolness is high on the list. For many years after I was totally unaware of that particular drama.

Paddy Joe's neighbours ensured that my visit remained unknown. They kept watch day and night and their diligence paid off. No one approached the house apart from the owner and family members, and after we had eaten we went to sleep. The days were taking their toll on my energy and I had to be fit for the next challenge. The following day was New Year's Eve. My hope was that we would celebrate New Year in County Monaghan. As we prepared to set off, a bottle of holy water from Knock was produced and sprinkled on us. We blessed ourselves and got into a car that had arrived to take us to an 'unapproved' road; these were used mostly by smugglers and would have less traffic. Two other cars would drive back and forward along the road to alert us in case of roadblocks or other police activity. At the appointed spot we alighted and the cars headed home.

Three of us set off on foot. The weather was absolutely Arctic and walking along the icy road was no easy task for me. Paddy Joe stayed with me while his brother Brendan walked ahead as lookout. If Brendan spotted anything he would

whistle and call his imaginary dog 'Spot' in a loud voice. This
happened several times and each time Paddy Joe and I jumped
from the road into the adjoining field. Every bone in my body
shook and the pain was unbearable as I had damaged all of the
discs – my shock absorbers – in my vertebrae. The worst pain
was in my heel and leg. It would take several years of
physiotherapy before the back pain disappeared. While walking
down a hill we heard a car coming around the corner behind
us. It moved at such speed that I was unable to jump off the
road in time. We decided to pretend we were smugglers, which
was a damn sight better than escapees. Just then the car slowed
and turned up a narrow hill road. 'That's the Brennans,' said
Paddy Joe, 'we're all right.'

At that point we decided to keep to the fields and bogs.
The ground was covered in snow and everything seemed
smooth on top but the snow was covering treacherous holes.
After a period of falling and scrambling back up again, I could
walk no further. Brendan and Paddy Joe placed their shoulders
under my armpits and they practically carried me the last few
miles of that perilous journey. We would stop from time to
time to survey the landscape as we feared a police platoon
might guess the possible crossing point and sit in ambush.
Seeing no movement, we continued on. Suddenly out of the
night and from behind thickets and trees came the shadows of
men making their way towards us. We hoped and prayed that
they were the men Paddy Joe had contacted in Monaghan. As
they approached us they called out Paddy Joe's name and
immediately surrounded us with the warmth of a great
welcome. We had made it! It was still 1960 for another hour
or so. I was free.

There was genuine delight and laughter as we trudged our
way across the invisible border. The feeling of elation that
consumed me was absolutely marvellous. My trials of the last
six days were over. We had beaten them despite the ring of
steel around Belfast and the biggest manhunt in the history of
the Six County state. People who had nothing to gain but a

lot to lose championed my cause. They literally risked life and livelihood to secure a safe passage for me into a new life of freedom. They live forever in my memory.

Some Courtesy Calls, Then on to Bundoran

We walked in jubilant mood towards a new two-storey house just yards from the border in Drumfurrer near Carrickroe. Peadar and Dympna Treanor welcomed us with open arms and we all sat down at a long table that had been set for the family to welcome in the New Year. The crowning presentation was a large cooked goose. The men had kept watch at the border for several hours. Their purpose was to ensure that the security forces did not attempt to snatch me at the last moment. They did their job well.

We celebrated our success. Due to my injuries I was unable to get into a car so, after our meal, Peadar placed an armchair in the back of his van to transport me further. I was whisked away to a house in Monaghan town owned by a Mrs Scallon and shown to a beautifully appointed bedroom where I slept a fitful sleep – my first real night of freedom since 1957. Once again I thought about John Kelly. Indeed, he was never far from my mind for many months afterwards. Paddy Joe also stayed that night before returning home the following morning. My injuries were really catching up on me now. The tortuous walk had reversed my slow improvement and my foot and leg hurt terribly. Paddy Joe O'Donnell and Dan Mullan collected me after breakfast and brought me to Monaghan General Hospital. I was not keen to stay there but nevertheless agreed to see a consultant who gave me medicine and arranged for a nurse to bandage my foot and leg. While we did not discuss how I sustained the injuries except to say a fall, he knew who he had in his rooms if only by the company I was in. He never spoke of it to the Gardaí.

We then made two courtesy calls at my request. The first was to see Vera Lanney, whose husband, Frank, was jailed for three years and was a great companion of mine. I called to see

Vera at the car tax office where she worked. As we departed she noticed someone looking at us very inquisitively whom she knew would go immediately to the Gardaí. Our second call was to the O'Hanlon family, whose son Feargal was killed along with Seán South in the attack on Brookeborough RUC Station on 1 January 1957. Feargal was our martyr and those of my age could identify closely with him and his family. Feargal's mother and sister Páidrigín were just coming out of the house on their way to his grave as it was the fourth anniversary of his death. They brought me inside to exchange greetings. I felt privileged to meet them.

After lunch in Scallons, Paddy and Dan arranged to bring me to my aunt Minnie who lived in Bundoran, County Donegal. While we were having lunch a messenger arrived with news that the local Garda superintendent was alleged to have said that the Gardaí knew I was in Monaghan town and that if an RUC Special Branch squad came over the border to get me the Gardaí would not stand in their way. It was a chilling message as I was aware of the vulnerability of being so close to the border. It was the first of many unwelcome interventions in my life from a specific section of the Gardaí. We consulted the map to ensure that the journey through the winding network of roads near the border from Monaghan to Bundoran did not expose us to being on the wrong side at any time. We arrived there safely. My aunt half expected me at some time and the welcome I got in St Enda's guesthouse made me feel at home immediately.

St Enda's was a ten-room house attached to another of similar style and architecture. The bay windows gave a view of traffic coming from the town and from the Sligo direction. The upstairs windows in the front had an unhindered view of the Atlantic with the waves crashing down on the golden sands. I was very debilitated after my travails and that was my principal reason for coming here. Aunt Minnie had been a matron at Bromsgrove Hospital in Birmingham during the Second World War and was considered by my family to have almost mythical powers for having restored my older brother Eugene back to life when he was only a baby. The following day was one of celebration because my parents, brothers and sister-in-law all arrived to greet me. Their pride was tangible. Every one of them had stories of being followed by the police and being questioned by journalists from the English newspapers. My parents told of how Paddy Joe McClean and another man called to the house two days before to say that I was safely across the border. Although the house in Omagh was being watched, as one would expect, the large number of well-wishers who called made identification by the police of anyone associated with the escape too difficult.

The following day the family whose support had made it all possible – the Kellys from Adela Street – arrived in strength to see me. They had stories of harassment, arrests, imprisonment and general badgering. The RUC knew they had helped me but did not know where I was. They searched rooms, attics, out-offices and neighbouring houses and generally turned many houses upside down. The family knew that John was not allowed visitors and was confined to a punishment cell with no bed during the day and reduced rations of food, which meant bread and water in place of some meals. It would be some months before John and I managed to re-establish contact.

Not long after my arrival in St Enda's I met Philip Donoghue, who was on the run as part of the last active IRA group on the Donegal/Tyrone/Fermanagh border. Phil was one of the lucky ones to escape the carnage at Brookeborough when Feargal O'Hanlon and Seán South were killed. My aunt's home was a safe house, a fact of which I was totally ignorant. This meant that for the short time I was lodged there, Phil and some comrades came and went. No one was ever traced to her house or arrested coming or going because she ran a tight ship.

Phil was in touch through his own channels with the IRA Chief of Staff and Director of Operations. He apprised them of my presence and they sent me a request to come to Dublin to meet them. Such a trip was not in my immediate plans nor had I intended to report back to the IRA, which was the convention for released and escapee prisoners. I had not been in the prison unit and therefore had no reason to pursue such a course. There was, however, one single motivation. I decided to respond positively to their invitation because John Kelly would have done so if he had succeeded in escaping. John would also be *persona non grata* with some of the IRA people in A Wing. Everyone likes to be associated with success so I knew the IRA would like to claim our achievement. If I was right, then John's position inside the prison would be much easier. The tiny minority who were angry with us would be deprived of any support by the fact that I had reported back to GHQ.

Reporting Back to GHQ – and a Sojourn in Tipperary

A few days later a car arrived at St Enda's to take me to Dublin. The driver was Owen Gough and he was accompanied by a lady called Eucharia Murray. We headed for Owen's house on Clonliffe Road in Drumcondra where I spent the night. During the night I was awakened to meet the IRA Chief of Staff, Ruairí Ó Brádaigh, and the newly appointed Director of Operations, Mick Ryan. They welcomed me warmly and spoke glowingly of how my escape improved morale generally. They never discussed why I was not part of the IRA prison unit, and were keen to look after my needs, such as lodgings. I told them I was returning to Bundoran and they invited me back to Dublin soon so that they could take care of me. The January edition of the republican newspaper, the *United Irishman*, carried the story of my escape, with a follow-up in the February edition. The leadership also issued an official statement.

A few weeks later I was collected by Owen and Eucharia and brought to Ruairí Ó Brádaigh's home in Longford where I stayed the night. His mother was also there. Ruairí drove me to Dublin where we met up with Cathal Goulding, who took over my care at this point. It was about this time that a specially organised IRA Convention decided to continue with the armed struggle despite the lack of money, arms and Volunteers. The decision was made at a critical time, as there were still hundreds in prison in the North. There had been major losses of arms captured by the security forces in both states and any member who had a government job (central or local) was summarily dismissed. Reliable sources reckoned that there were as few as sixteen active service Volunteers at this time. Support from the US had dried up with the growing realisation that Operation Harvest was not going to succeed in its aims, but it was not for another year that the campaign was finally called off following the introduction of the Military Courts by Minister for Justice, Charles Haughey. These courts handed down eight-year sentences for offences that previously merited only six months.

Cathal Goulding brought me to a house in Fairview belonging to Mr and Mrs Sheeran who lived there with their son, Tommy, and his wife, Bernadette, and young baby. There was a lovely atmosphere in the house. The Sheerans fed me and housed me free of charge and treated me like a VIP. I stayed in a number of such houses over the following five months before eventually setting out on my own. Although there was no warrant out for my arrest, Cathal thought it better that I stay in the shadows as much as possible, and to avoid attention I was moved around. My next house was in Shanard Road in Santry with Gay and Des Wilson and their young son, Fergus, who became lifelong friends. All this time my injuries continued to give me serious pain.

Cathal Goulding was at this time Quartermaster General (QMG) of the IRA. A small fair-haired man with the look of eternal youth, as QMG he knew where every gun and bullet was hidden throughout the country. He had been sentenced to eight years in 1953 for a raid on an army officer training corps school in England. He succeeded Ruairí Ó Brádaigh as

Chief of Staff in 1962. In the 1970s he became the leader of the Official IRA and led his group to form the Workers' Party.

Cathal called one day in his Morris Minor to take me to Tipperary. Our destination was Ballymackey, to the house of a republican named Dan Gleeson. My family had a connection with this part of the country as my grandaunt had emigrated to America and married a man named Duff from near Toomevara. Dan, his wife Maureen and daughter Áine made me welcome in their cosy farmhouse up a winding lane with a clear view of the 'Devil's Bit'. As it was springtime Dan was busy on the farm. He had been advised by Cathal Goulding to keep knowledge of my presence confined to trusted republicans.

Dan was steeped in republicanism. His family had suffered during the War of Independence and the Civil War and Dan had been interned in the Curragh Camp in the 1940s and again in 1957. During my time in Tipperary I answered job advertisements in the *Irish Independent* and must have written 100 letters seeking employment because I did not want to be a burden on such generous folk. I did not receive one reply and so decided to return to Dublin. It was clear to me at this point that there was no longer any justification for me being on the run. The IRA had looked after me by leaving me in the country to recuperate and it was now time for me to look after myself.

13

LIFE AFTER INCARCERATION

The Humphreys and My Early Years in Cork

When I was in Crumlin Road a well-known Dublin family 'adopted' me as someone to correspond with and support. They wrote to me and sent me books and magazines. They were Emmet and Evelyn Humphreys from Ailesbury Road. Evelyn's first letter quoted from her cousin Dora Sigerson Shorter's poem on the 'rebels' of 1916: 'They lit a fire within the land and have enkindled it with their hearts of gold.' Emmet and his brother Dick had been active in the national struggle for many years, while their sister Síghle was also an unrepentant republican.

The Humphreys invited me to stay and I did so for several weeks. There were many callers, such as Evelyn's brother, the well-known Irish language author Donn Piatt, as well as 'Mac', who had inherited the title of 'The O'Rahilly' and his wife Elgin, a sister of Kevin Barry, executed in 1920 at the age of eighteen.

My next move was to Blarney Street in Cork to the home of Donnacha and Christine Ó Murchú who had invited me. I had spent holidays there before being imprisoned so knew the area fairly well. Donnacha was a teacher of high standing in Cork's famous North Mon, a Christian Brothers school on the northside of the city. A committed member of Sinn Féin, he had visited Mid-Ulster during the three elections there in the mid-1950s, where we first met. Christine had a shop that was a feature of its time in Cork. It was in the front sitting room of the house on Blarney Street and had every type and colour of wool ever created. The shop door was also the main door into the house and that meant callers had to go through the shop to access the living room.

Donnacha brought me to Dr Kiely, who recommended X-rays and subsequent outpatient treatment for my leg in the North Infirmary. I was keen to put my injuries behind me but was unaware that the bigger problem was in my back. Almost every day Donncha introduced me to someone new. One of the first I met was Jim O'Regan, who had been jailed in English prisons for ten years during and after the Second World War for his involvement in the Seán Russell-led IRA bombing campaign in England. Jim lived in Sunday's Well and came from a reasonably well-off family. I was a frequent visitor to his home.

We had been envious of the Cork lads in Crumlin Road as several priests used to make an annual pilgrimage from home to visit them. One of those was an t-Athair Tadhg Ó Murchú. A fluent Irish speaker, he encouraged the use of the language at all times. He and Donnacha had much the same commitment to the fostering of the language and it was not long before he called to Blarney Street to meet me. He invited me to his parochial house in Carrignavar on a kind of a holiday and I spent a great week there. An t-Athair Tadhg was the epitome of a good Christian. He travelled to various prisons to meet the inmates and always tried to help ex-prisoners find employment.

In the spring 1972 edition of the magazine *An Sagart* ('The Priest'), Fr Tomás Ó Fiaich (later Archbishop of Armagh and Cardinal Primate) referred to an t-Athair Tadhg's connections with ex-prisoners. He wrote that he had contacts far and wide and a humorous tale is told of an t-Athair Tomás

Ó Flannachadha who visited the parochial house every Friday night. On one occasion when an t-Athair Tomás called, who was sitting in the chair beside the fire chatting to an t-Athair Tadhg but Danny Donnelly, the escaped prisoner. On another Friday night who was sitting in the same chair but the Garda Commissioner himself!

I did not receive any money from the republican movement as their US source had dried up and I was very anxious at this stage to find employment and stand on my own two feet. But with the introduction of the Military Courts this became even more difficult. I had to tell potential employers about my background because if I did not, more than likely someone else would, resulting in almost certain dismissal. The Special Branch of the Gardaí specialised in this tactic. When at one stage I did obtain a modest job two detectives arrived at the office in Rocksavage to inform my employers of my status.

One day I walked in to City Hall and when I asked to see the Lord Mayor, Stephen Barrett, a Fine Gael councillor, I was immediately granted an audience. I told him who I was (he had read about me) and explained that I was finding it difficult to get a job. He promised to make a few calls. He was a man of his word, and I received a letter from him within three days. In it he referred me to Séamus Fitzgerald, a Fianna Fáil councillor who had a thriving electrical business on South Mall. Séamus had been involved in the 'Tan War' and had strong republican credentials. I told him I would be able for clerical work, and within a week I was invited to an interview at the Irish International Trading Corporation in Rocksavage, an import/export business providing salt to every creamery in Munster. Its wholesale hardware section was an increasing part of the operation. I got a job there earning £5 a week.

Not having any form of transport and being some distance from the job, I moved into digs at Mrs Hegarty's on Evergreen Road, where I remained for the rest of my time in Cork, a period of over two years. Within the month Mrs Hegarty was visited by two Special Branch detectives who apprised her of my identity. They asked about my movements and who called to see me. It was the first of several visits – but they never came to question me. They did the same thing at my new place of work. I understood very quickly that it was a form of harassment.

As I had so little money I spent my spare time in the Crawford School of Art, which was free, and became an ardent fan of sculpture and artwork of every kind. On other occasions I would take a bus to Blarney, Crosshaven or Cobh on Sundays when there were no football or hurling matches in the Athletic Grounds (now Páirc Uí Chaoimh). I am privileged to say that I saw the great Christy Ring play on many occasions between 1961 and 1963. Meanwhile in Crumlin Road Gaol the news that I was in Cork gave rise to banter between prisoners and warders. Every morning for a period when the warder in charge would shout out to his superior the number of prisoners walking in the yard, a prisoner would add 'and one in Cork' until Class Officer Woods would himself shout 'Sixty-nine correct, Sir – and one in Cork' to deprive Frank McArdle of his heckle.

Making Progress – and Some Important Initiatives

My work colleagues in the small office were very supportive of me and we had great banter. During this time my leg and ankle were healing but the pain in my back was becoming intolerable. A local doctor advised me to see the consultant Dr St John McConnell, who diagnosed that the cartilages in my vertebrae had been damaged by the fall and recommended attendance at the Cork Polio Clinic. He considered my injuries significant and not helped by the passage of time. He told me that a complete restoration was unlikely but that my age was in my favour. Irish International Trading permitted time off on two afternoons a week for several weeks while I attended the clinic on South Mall. The staff there had built their experience and wonderful reputation on the two unfortunate outbreaks of polio in Cork which devastated the city in the

1950s. I am deeply indebted to them also because, over a relatively short space of time, they brought about a complete recovery.

By this time I had developed a new set of friends in Cork city, including my fellow lodgers and work colleagues. I also had the good fortune to meet Paddy and Jean Crowley who lived in Turners Cross. Their home became a regular calling house and my parents were frequent guests there when they visited me in Cork. On Saturday nights we played cards with their respective mothers and sometimes brothers and sisters. In retrospect this was better for me than any counselling. Paddy, Jean and their baby son Ciarán provided me with a real sense of family.

Counselling was a term not heard in those days. People suffered traumas and went to work the next day. For some it worked but for many their traumas dogged their lives. Modern living has placed an importance on counselling which has undoubtedly brought many benefits to people who have survived a traumatic experience. I had been incarcerated for over three years and had faced great challenges in my escape. Carrying those injuries for three months without any hospital treatment and being totally dependant on other people for lodgings and food created all kinds of conflicts in my mind. My real wish was to be independent.

Many former prisoners have told me how they found it exceptionally difficult to re-adjust to life on the outside. Prisoners are 'institutionalised' when inside – their meals are served, their clothes washed and they are told what to do and shepherded everywhere they go. They lose all their independence. On being released they are suddenly faced with having to make decisions once again. Relating to strangers can be extremely trying, while paranoia is a common feeling in the early months. For those with little or no adult experience of the outside world, establishing friendships is not an easy task. This was something the republican movement never acknowledged or even discussed. No group was in a better

position than them to create an understanding of the
psychological challenges that face ex-prisoners. There was no
initiative to provide counselling. Their inaction is a mystery
to me and has cost many an ex-prisoner dearly.

During this time a Dublin businessman called Pádraig Ó
Síocháin started an Irish language organisation to create
friendship in business through the use of Irish. He named it
CARA, the Irish for 'friend'. Paddy Crowley invited me to
join and we used to meet in the Metropole Hotel on a
monthly basis. Pádraig Ó Síocháin is practically forgotten now
but he was a one-man band drumming up business for Irish
goods and particularly those made in the Gaeltacht. Pádraig
supplied my prison colleague Frank McArdle with many Irish
language books to assist them in their Irish classes in the
prison.

Paddy and Jean also introduced me to Críostoir de Baróid,
who had embarked on a venture called Scéim na
gCeardcumann (Trade Union Scheme) focused on returning
the Irish language to the ordinary working people. It was an
idea reminiscent of the cultural resurgence in late nineteenth-
century Ireland that saw the birth of the GAA and Conradh
na Gaeilge. Scéim na gCeardcumann was a well thought out
idea structured around the twin pillars of culture and
education. The cultural side featured a range of people who
worked voluntarily, including Pádraig Tyers of Gael Linn and
Seán Ó Sé, arguably the most recognised singer of national
songs of his generation. Críostóir also had a section named the
Mionscoil, a series of lectures on economic and national
interest. This 'little university' was a source of education for
everyone, especially those who might not have had as much
formal education as others.

Ar Lorg na Laoch

The historical education aspect of the scheme was entitled Ar
Lorg na Laoch, loosely translated as 'In the Footsteps of our
Heroes'. This was a most timely and important initiative. Many

of the men and women who fought in the Black and Tan War were still alive and living in and around Cork. The wonderful aspect of this programme was the willingness of the participants to be involved. Large groups of us went by bus to the ambush sites in the west of the county. During that period I met Tom Barry and his second in command, Tom Kelleher, who was a customer of ours in Irish International Trading. Both had fought in west Cork against the British forces and had great success at both Crossbarry and Kilmichael. It has been revealed by historians that the British decision to sue for a truce with the IRA in 1921 was due to the activities of Tom Barry's flying column, particularly after Crossbarry. Despite being surrounded by 1,200 troops and the hated Auxiliaries, the force of 100 IRA escaped after inflicting heavy casualties. Thirty-nine British were killed and forty wounded with only four casualties for the IRA. The real lesson was that a guerilla force of such determination working in the geographical environment of west Cork among a mostly supportive population could not be defeated easily.

Another large personality of the period was Major Florence (Florrie) O'Donoghue whom I met with his wife, Josephine. Florrie was Head of Intelligence for the Cork Brigade of the IRA while Josephine was a clerk to the British Major in charge of Cork. Josephine had married a Welshman who died young, leaving her with two young sons. His family, the Marchments, had not approved of the marriage, mainly on religious grounds. Their prejudices were given full rein after their son's death and they insisted on retaining the couple's older son at their home in Wales when Josephine had returned to Cork. A subsequent court case gave the grandparents custody, much to Josephine's anguish. In Cork, however, she met Fr Albert at the Holy Trinity Capuchin Church, who promised her she would see her son soon in Ireland. He went directly to the Cork IRA who abducted the child and brought him back to Ireland where he was kept in a safe house until the 1921 Truce. The man who organised the abduction was

Florrie O'Donoghue. While the plot was being hatched Josephine ensured that a copy of every note that went through British Army Headquarters in Cork went to Florrie first. Her work for Irish freedom was incalculable. Josephine and Florrie later married and had four other children.

In just over two years I had made a number of good friends, too numerous to mention here, who made my new life in Cork a seminal experience. The only drawback was that my wages were low, just £7 10s per week. The average wage was £10 and I knew that my best chance of advancement was a move to Dublin. Before leaving Cork I was the recipient of two formal presentations, one at work and the other at Scéim na gCeardcumann; it overwhelmed me that people could be so kind and generous. It made my departure from Cork all the more difficult.

14

A Business Life

Beginning a New Phase in Dublin

In spring 1963 I spotted an article by Terry O'Sullivan in the *Evening Press* about the annual dinner dance of a company named Urney Chocolates in Tallaght, County Dublin. The part that caught my eye was that the Assistant Managing Director, Arthur Behan, gave his speech in Irish. I knew that Urney was a village near Strabane on the Tyrone/Donegal border, so there was probably a Tyrone connection. That night I wrote a letter of application in Irish for a job in Urneys. To my delight I received a reply from Arthur Behan, also in Irish, inviting me for interview. At the time Tallaght was a village of a couple of hundred homes but boasted three factories on the Belgard Road. One of those was Urney Chocolates, which employed a thousand people.

I took the bus from Dublin city to Newland's Cross and then a long walk to Urneys. I was interviewed by Arthur Behan and the personnel manager, Seán Murray. Much of the interview was in Irish and I was introduced to the purchasing manager, Paddy Butler, originally from Dundrum in Tipperary, who would prove to be a great influence in my life. I was appointed assistant to Paddy on condition that I took a course in business studies. This I did at night at Rathmines College of

Commerce where I successfully completed exams over the next three years. Paddy and his wife, Sheila, became close family friends and were godparents to our eldest daughter, Úna.

Half of Urney Chocolates was purchased in 1963 by the American W. R. Grace Company, which had a huge shipping operation in South America. The owner was Peter Grace, whose parents hailed from Kilkenny. Urneys was fortunate to have as its Managing Director Tommy Headon, a man of vision and courage with a huge number of contacts. He expanded the company, taking over Devlin's of Cork Street, R. H. Steele's in Blackrock and Murch and Pascal's in England. It was an exciting time in Ireland as the plans for economic expansion were being developed and export business was booming. I spent eleven great years at Urney Chocolates.

Grace Brothers eventually bought the other half of Urneys but in 1980 needed to encash their European investments and sold ice cream companies they owned in Denmark and Ireland (which included HB Ice Cream in Rathfarnham) to Unilever. Unilever is a multinational company and at that time employed almost 300,000 people worldwide. It was the beginning of the end for Urneys which, after sixty years of business and although still making profits, was closed and the land sold in 1986.

It was during my time in Urneys that I understood the lengths to which some bosses would go to bend workers to their will. A new set of directors came in when Grace Brothers took full control. They brought with them their own middle management team, mostly recent graduates, who were used to destabilise the older management structure. In the early 1970s I was appointed credit controller to reduce extended credit terms for customers. I was given a new office with an old desk, inside which I found a memo. Its contents were most disconcerting. Written by the Personnel Director to all other directors both national and foreign, it proposed that events should be manipulated in such a way that Urneys' staff would have no option but to go on strike. The proposal continued that the company's best interests would be served if workers in the other two major Dublin confectionery firms, Rowntree's and Cadbury's, could be enticed to join the Urneys workers in their strike. The issue chosen to ignite the strike should be a peripheral one, well in advance of the upcoming wage round. The thinking was that the trade unions involved would be lumbered with strike pay and would be more easily dealt with when negotiations started on the next wage round.

When news broke of Unilever's intention to sell or close Urneys in 1974 the workers called for strike action and to extend picketing to the other Unilever factories in Ireland. In those years a union picket was obeyed by almost everyone, even when the reason given was most unfair. Many of the older workers were concerned about the real motivation of some of the trade union members who were urging a strike. The younger members of staff were being encouraged to make a macho display and bring the new owner 'to its senses'. But the reality was that a strike at that time would have made it easy for the new owners to close the factory.

A general meeting was held in the canteen in the Belgard Road factory. Mattie Merrigan led the Amalgamated Trade Union fearlessly on behalf of the workers. Mattie was one of the wisest trade union leaders of his time, and with people like Charlie Douglas and Jimmy Tinkler represented what was best about unions. When workers needed someone to speak up for them these men went above and beyond the call of duty to ensure fair play. Mattie chaired the meeting in the canteen, which was crowded with hundreds of workers. Some speeches were made to galvanise support for strike action and were received with great acclaim. Timing is a most important factor in most events and I had to choose the most opportune moment to speak. Most managers were not in any union so there were very few colleagues with me. The mood was certainly for strike and the proposal was that a strike should be called immediately and pickets placed on all Unilever enterprises in the country. I asked to speak and Mattie called for silence.

Having had time to understand the issues and having been alerted to the dangers, I had worked out a proposal that I knew could have massive support if I got a good hearing. I started with a description of the Urneys factory established some sixty years earlier in a village setting in Tallaght, one that had given workers in the surrounding districts from Blessington to Walkinstown a great livelihood. It helped them educate their children and provided funds for a house and a car. I pointed out that it was a strong, vibrant company that had attracted interest from the American giant Grace Brothers, who eventually purchased the entire operation. The point was that we needed to persuade Unilever that Urneys could survive because it had a great record. My proposal was to avoid a strike as it would give the wrong message about the company and a false picture of the workers and, just as importantly, workers could ill afford to lose their wages over a period of time. There was also a risk that the strike would make it easier for the owners to sell.

I proposed that members of the union shop committee should be divided into two teams, one of which would go to Unilever headquarters in Rotterdam and the other to Leinster House. Our appeal should be presented to the international board in Rotterdam and publicity sought from the media. All costs would be paid for by the workforce contributing one week's wages. The second team should seek an audience with Justin Keating, Minister for Trade and Industry, and again publicity about the positive aspects of the company sought. The minister would have been very supportive of our cause. Finally I proposed that our story should be printed on a single A4 sheet and distributed at all Unilever factories in Ireland simultaneously with the two delegations. The other Unilever workers should be informed that this was an information picket only and should be requested to continue to work but to support our case.

Mattie was delighted with my proposal as he always took Jim Larkin's view that a strike was the last option that should be exercised. The entire assembly acclaimed the proposal with loud cheers and it was overwhelmingly passed when Mattie put it to a vote.

The following day Mattie and the union representatives were informed by Unilever that as chocolate was not their core business they did not want the factory but would keep it open for five years with a view to selling it eventually or closing it at a date after that time. It was the best we could do. When the factory finally closed in 1980 the highest recorded redundancy package at the time was paid to the 300 remaining workers.

In 1974, having seen the writing on the wall, I had transferred to the HB Ice Cream plant in Rathfarnham. HB Ice Cream was an offshoot of Hughes Dairies founded by the Hughes family of Hazelbrook in 1926 as an addition to their bottled milk business. Most of the milk businesses in Dublin discovered that making ice cream was the most convenient and profitable method of dealing with surplus milk supplies. The Irish owners did not recognise the potential of ice cream, but when Grace Brothers took over they bought state of the art machines from Denmark and the US and built a new factory in Rathfarnham in 1966. It was the first of its kind in Ireland and established ice cream manufacture as a very profitable and growing business. In their first year at the new plant they sold 2 million gallons of ice cream, growing by another million within a short space of time.

The Irish-owned milk companies combined to create Premier Dairies in Rathfarnham and HB Ice Cream went on to become the most prestigious brand in the country, which it remains to this day. In 1974 Unilever purchased HB Ice Cream as part of their strategy to create a pan-European ice cream brand. They also bought Hellerup in Denmark, Wall's in the UK, Langnese in Germany and eventually every major ice cream brand and factory in Europe. I joined the Rathfarnham

team in 1974 as Irish food business purchasing manager. The
Irish part of Unilever expanded, taking over the frozen food
brand Bird's Eye and building depots throughout the country
from Tralee to Sligo.

Representing Workers' Rights

I very sensibly continued my union membership although
neither HB managers nor clerical supervisors were unionised
in any way. Then against all the odds a strike took place in
1984 over residual matters arising from a previous one in 1981.
Most of the issues over the years arose in relation to our van
salesmen who did a most outstanding and pressurised job.
Instead of being treasured, the Dublin-based salesmen felt they
were being treated with hostility. I knew them as dedicated
men who never wanted to be on strike as it deprived them of
money for their families. I was of the opinion that the problem
lay with management, who were clearly not managing the
workforce properly.

In 1984 the 'all-out picket' was a comparatively recent
Congress of Trade Unions directive designed to end the anxiety
around passing an unofficial picket. It was a clever rule as a
company had to pay anyone who turned up for work, which
sometimes meant doing very little, so the pressure to resolve an
issue was turned back on management. Despite our hopes, the
day of the all-out picket arrived and I stayed away. Almost
immediately I received a call to return my company car. I was
somewhat isolated as I was the only member of management
who was in a union. As the strike proceeded without any end
in sight I decided to sign on for social welfare payments. I
signed on for two weeks but never got any money as the strike
ended unexpectedly, to our great relief. Returning to work on
foot with a close neighbour and colleague, we walked into the
Director's office to collect the keys of our company cars, which
were returned to us immediately. On entering the canteen later
that morning we received a great cheer. The news that we had
resisted the enormous pressure to return to work by having

our company cars taken had circulated widely and ordinary workers were both incensed by the heavy hand of the company and appreciative of our support.

Unilever's business in Ireland increased substantially and my responsibilities also grew to include planning. They had two major manufacturing plants, one in Rathfarnham and the other in Drogheda. Some 50 per cent of the company's turnover is in food products and the other half in personal products and detergents. They treat their employees well. Their training programmes are always finely tuned to improve the skills of their managers and other workers and no one is excluded from knowledge about the company, its strategy and its performance.

In 1994 a directive from the European Union made it obligatory for transnational companies with 150 workers in two or more countries and employing more than 1,000 workers to create a European Works Council within two years or have one imposed on them. The European Works Council would be created from the elected or appointed representatives from each country, with Unilever Ireland entitled to one representative. The purpose of the council was to provide a mechanism for these major companies to consult and inform their workers of trends, changes and plans. The person elected would represent all employees from the factory floor to the boardroom. It was almost a foregone conclusion that our representative would be a SIPTU member, as it was the largest union both within the company and in the country. Nevertheless, my name was put forward.

The Personnel Director convened a meeting of all candidates to agree the method of election and how to ensure that all employees countrywide would be aware of each candidate's credentials. It was agreed that a photograph and two-sentence description of each candidate would be distributed to every employee. As regards voting, despite my protests the method chosen was first past the post rather than proportional representation.

My initial aim was to come second behind the SIPTU candidate. My first task was to highlight my qualifications and outline how I would follow up on issues arising out of the consultation and information process. A national forum of seven people with representation from all unions and all factories and offices would be created to advise me. This was an important promise as it guaranteed the workers that even though I was a manager I was going to represent everyone. These proposals were set out on a black-and-white printed circular that I paid for myself. All Unilever employees countrywide received one. There were four other candidates, all attached to a trade union.

On 5 October 1995 it was announced that I had received the most votes and would represent all Unilever workers in Ireland in the first ever Unilever European Works Council. At the first meetings of the council my recurring question concerned the investment plans for Ireland for the following year. The Unilever executive presiding, Tony Burgmanns (later Chairman of the company), made a point of inviting me to share his table at lunch as obviously he could not understand how a manager could be voted into such a position by the unionised workers. We debated the rumoured strategy of Unilever wishing to close factories and centralise manufacturing in a selected number of countries. My point was that the company had the best return on capital employed, the best profits, the highest turnover and factories with the strongest local roots of any competitor – so why change it?

When I retired from Unilever in 1998 I also handed over my Unilever European Works Council Representative position to a colleague, elected by the national forum, who was a member of SIPTU. Works councils are most definitely a crucial step forward in the advancement of workers' involvement, but it is vital that the concept is fully understood and their limitations recognised. Despite having such a forum, Unilever, in the years that followed, reduced their number of brands from 1,600 to 400 and their workforce to 174,000 with

factories closed in Italy, Holland, Belgium, Greece and Ireland
as they sought the cheaper labour markets of eastern Europe.
In recent years they offloaded Bird's Eye, which Irish
management had developed into a multi-million pound
business with great benefits for local processors. There is now
no trace of either of the two large, bustling manufacturing
plants, either in Tallaght or Rathfarnham, where I spent most
of my working life. Only the brands survive, which goes to
show that, in the eyes of multinationals, brands are more
important than factories or people.

Professional Skills and International Contacts

In 1971 I was invited by the Council of the Institute of
Purchasing and Materials Management to become the
Honorary Secretary. I succeeded Brian Maguire, who had
been a captain in the Irish Army and my predecessor as
Engineering Buyer for Urney Chocolates. The institute is
essentially an educational body providing courses for new
buyers. On taking up my position as Honorary Secretary I
planned a development strategy with the voluntary board
which resulted in the Institute becoming the recognised centre
of competence for the profession. I held the position of
Secretary for several years as well as other voluntary roles. In
my opinion it is almost obligatory for professionals to involve
themselves with their recognised professional body as so many
new initiatives surface through international and academic
contacts which slowly revolutionise the way we operate. Many
very competent and skilled people, like my close colleagues
John Hickson and Noel McInerney, gave their time
voluntarily towards building up a relevant and effective
national organisation. On two occasions I was elected
President of the Institute, which was a marvellous opportunity
to promote the contribution that talented buyers can make to
Irish industry.

With Joe O'Connor of Harrington, Goodlass Wall Paints
as President, I developed international links through a new

organisation known as the International Federation. This expanded the knowledge base and was a harbinger of the development that would take place both socially and commercially with the increasing role of the Common Market. We were ahead of most other organisations with our connections not only in Europe but throughout the world. As senior delegate I met with many of the leading protagonists and academics who were setting the trends and identifying the skills necessary to bring about progress in the field of negotiation, sourcing and chain of supply. I spent most of my working life as a negotiator, and with the support and vision of our Managing Director, Ted Murphy, and his board we created many opportunities for Irish companies to benefit financially and commercially. We worked closely with the Industrial Development Authority (IDA) and Córas Tráchtála in establishing new industries in Ireland. Irish suppliers were wonderful assets and many of my successes on behalf of Unilever were due to their dedication, ingenuity and innovation. On occasions sharp demands were made on them as we tried to push down costs but once the suppliers were made part of the project, success was almost assured. They were exciting times but nothing gave as much satisfaction as being able to source products from local Irish companies because this generated employment and kept money in the country. We cooperated with the Irish Goods Council which did so much good under the direction of Vivian Murray and John Corrigan.

At a conference in Mexico in 1977 I secured the Fourth International World Congress for Dublin, to be held in 1983. This would be attended by hundreds of buyers whose spending budgets were colossal. It was a difficult time in Ireland with high unemployment and national debt, so hosting such a congress was a good opportunity to promote the profile of the country to foreign decision makers. Securing the congress was a hard fight and was only achieved with the help of Irish-American delegate Frank Winters. The event proved a huge success, with President Patrick Hillery impressing all the delegates enormously with his wide international knowledge. To see and hear him operate was an education in itself.

In 1998, during my last period as President of the Institute I was invited to the annual dinner of our sister organisation in the UK. It was a formal affair in London with an attendance of mostly men. As President of a national organisation, I was given the honour of being seated at the top table. There were seven of us at that table and all but three were Knights of the Realm. Beside me was Lieutenant General Sir Robert Hayman-Joyce, Deputy Head of the British Department of Defence Procurement. He was a very well informed man and asked me immediately about my views on the anticipated Bloody Sunday enquiry. I told him that the Lord Widgery enquiry was regarded as a complete whitewash and that the new enquiry was inevitable. The main speaker was Sir Clement Freud, a grandson of the famous psychoanalyst Sigmund Freud. Clement served in the Royal Ulster Rifles during the Second World War. He was at one time an aide to Field Marshall Montgomery and also assisted at the Nazi trials in Nuremburg.

Across the table Sir Clement asked me what part of Ireland I was from. I told him Dublin but originally from the North. Immediately he said, while locking his eyes on mine in that focused way of his, 'I fought for you during the war, you know.' 'Where did you fight for me, Sir Clement?' I asked. 'In Omagh,' came the reply. When I told him Omagh was my home town he asked me if I knew of Killyclogher. Of course I did and I ventured that it was some feat to remember the name some fifty years later. 'I have good reason to remember it,' he replied. 'I lost my virginity there.' He then added that some years previously he had mentioned this on Northern Ireland radio and had received twenty letters from women claiming to have been that woman!

Then I decided to tell a story about a curate in Omagh

named Dr Marren. In those days some priests were obsessed with stamping out the practice of people standing at the back of the church. On one occasion, not long after the Battle of Dunkirk when 350,000 British soldiers were evacuated from the beaches of Normandy, Dr Marren asked those standing at the back of the church to come up the aisles and take their seats. Among the crowd were a number of British soldiers. Some of the local people, with great embarrassment, followed the priest's instructions while others scarpered out the door. The soldiers continued to stand their ground, however. After the third command to come up the church Dr Marren announced with great solemnity, 'His Majesty the King will be delighted to hear that the British Army has taken a stand at last.' No one at the table laughed.

When he rose to speak Sir Clement gave me a look to say that he was going to get me back for that story. Not long into his oration, which was packed with humorous anecdotes that showed no respect for age, sex or race, he announced that his table had the honour of having the President of the Irish Institute which, he said, reminded him of a story. To the 500-strong audience he recounted his tale. A man was attracted by a poster advertising a holiday for two weeks in the Bahamas for £20. He immediately thought, 'I'll have that', paid his £20 and as he took his ticket was hit over the head with a heavy instrument. He woke up to find himself in chains in a rowing boat with a slave driver lashing him with a whip. He looked around and saw a man beside him. The man was Irish. He said to him, 'I hope they at least fly us home', to which the Irishman replied, 'Well, they didn't last year!' Sir Clement looked over at me, delighted that he had got his revenge.

15

PEADAR AND LILE O'DONNELL AND THE COOPERATIVE MOVEMENT

In spring 1963 I read a review Peadar O'Donnell's book *There Will Be Another Day*. The review featured an extract which told of Peadar's speech in Nenagh in response to Bishop Joseph Fogarty's alleged expulsion of a clerical student due to the politics of the young man's father. It was explosive. The book had everything – revolution, confrontation with the Empire, manipulation, intrigue, small farmers to whom I could relate and great writing. I had only known vaguely of Peadar O'Donnell but this book encouraged me to learn more. When I moved to Dublin I was asked if I would like to meet Peadar and his wife Lile (née O'Donel) at their home on Drumcondra Road. We had an immediate connection. His attitude to life, his sense of humour, his critical approach to most issues and his personal values all mirrored mine. We had both experienced the hardship of prison and of escaping and, more importantly, we both prided ourselves in having a keen sense of justice. We became lifelong friends.

Lile was as radical as Peadar and in many ways more discerning. She went to finishing school in Switzerland, spoke French fluently and toured the Greek islands as part of her education. She was articulate and wise, and so sure of herself she would challenge the Pope if necessary. I fondly recall

Sunday mornings after Mass gathered with others in their
house with Lile as master of ceremonies. The room would
hum with debates on all sorts of topics, especially current
government policies. There was always a coterie of twenty-
and thirty-year-olds, brought mainly by me.

Peadar, who was seventy when I first met him, was heavily
involved at this time with an initiative that gave great hope to
small farmers and men and women of no property. It was
known as the Glencolumbkille Project. The enterprise was
initiated by Fr James McDyer from Glenties, County Donegal,
who worked as a curate in Glencolumbkille in southwest
Donegal in the 1950s. Peadar and Lile spent their summers in
Dungloe and were well aware of the social potential of a
successful cooperative in the area. Lt General Michael Joe
Costello, former head of the state-owned Irish Sugar
Company and later supremo at Erin Foods, became involved,
as did Peadar O'Donnell, who saw the enterprise as
representing a marvellous opportunity to bring immediate
assistance to the local population and show up the
government's years of neglect of small farmers.

The Glencolumbkille Cooperative was set up in 1961.
While the powers of organisation and persuasion of Fr
McDyer were critical to its success, the involvement of
General Costello was the key. Costello's Erin Foods representatives set out the procedure for planting and cultivating
vegetables and demonstrated the yield per ton per acre of
individual vegetable types. The most crucial part of this
presentation was the price available to the small farmer for the
various vegetables, a price guaranteed by Erin Foods. For the
first time small farmers were promised a guaranteed market
and highly remunerative price for vegetables. It was
revolutionary. This was not in accordance with government
policy, which was more in tune with the Common Market's
view that small farmers were a burden to be disposed of.
Accordingly, the Department of Finance and various
government agencies set about creating obstacles in an attempt
to scupper the cooperative idea.

During my regular visits to Peadar we hatched a plan to replicate Glencolumbkille in as many places along the western seaboard as possible. We were determined not to become a smokescreen for government neglect but to use the cooperatives' success to highlight this neglect and force the government to take positive action. We formed a group initially comprised of Urney Chocolates employees – managerial, supervisory and factory floor volunteers – and started out by showing a film of the Glencolumbkille project that had been made by RTÉ. After each film we had a panel discussion that usually included Peadar. He was a great draw, and wherever we went in Dublin several hundred attended. The purpose was to galvanise public opinion to force the government to create real investment in the western counties.

We formed Dóchas Cooperative, which became the urban end of a very articulate and increasingly influential western lobby. Peadar had an ability to secure support from the most unusual places, and we secured patronage from influential people in business, agriculture and the Church. Our urban group assisted with several indigenous developments in Kilcrohane, west Cork, and Ballyvaughan, County Clare, and the plan was to have a dozen or so pilot schemes along the west coast that would highlight the extent of government neglect over the years.

We decided to forge an alliance between the industrial worker and the small farm countryside and so brought the case to the trade union movement, which was fully supportive. Under Peadar's influence and direction we engaged the Department of Agriculture in public debate, a sign that we were being taken seriously and that the politicians were worried. Meetings were held throughout the country, one of the largest being in Charlestown, County Mayo, featuring Bishop Browne of Galway, John Feeley of the Irish Creamery Milk Suppliers' Association (ICMSA) and Seán McEvoy of the Save the West campaign which represented many small farmers.

Out of the blue I had a call summoning me to a meeting with the Minister for Finance, Charles Haughey. Peadar counselled that anyone leading an agitation must never attend such a meeting alone, so accompanying me to the meeting were Lile O'Donnell, Caitríona McConnell and Adrian Gallagher. We emphasised the importance of people and how local cooperatives should be assisted by the government and highlighted the benefits for all of a well-populated, prosperous countryside. During the meeting we compared the financial investment in industry with the total lack of assistance for communities in the west. Mr Haughey almost sneered as he said, 'I suppose you are going to drag up Potez again,' referring to a major controversy at the time involving grants awarded by the IDA to a failed enterprise, Potez Aerospace, on the Naas Road. My reply took the wind out of his sails. 'No, we do not criticise the Potez venture because it failed. The Potez factory is a sign that someone at least tried. There is no similar grand wreckage anywhere in the small farm countryside nor specifically in the west to show that anyone tried anything.' It was vintage Peadar O'Donnell, whom I was quoting, but I took ownership of it myself on this occasion. Mr Haughey was immediately on our side. There was a recognition that we had a strategy and a policy that was independent of just embarrassing the government.

Within weeks he announced a Special West Fund of £100,000 in which he created a new post of Development Officer for several counties. Our organisation was practically made redundant. Kilcrohane Cooperative, the first one that we were associated with, went on to become a great success, while Ballyvaughan in County Clare was another beacon of hope. As west Cork enjoys a mild winter climate it was realised that they could grow daffodils and tulips well in advance of competitors in other European countries and succeeded in creating markets in Wales and even in Holland. In 1975 we visited Kilcrohane Cooperative and were very impressed by their production and packing lines and their brand name,

'Bantry Bay Flowers'. The cooperative survived until the 1990s. Not long after the creation of the Special West Fund Mr Haughey increased the amount to £250,000 and extended the Development Officers to twelve counties. It was recognition of the campaign's efforts and proved what Peadar O'Donnell always claimed – that people power could move mountains if effectively planned and applied.

About this time I was planning to marry Caitríona McConnell from Cabra whom I met in March 1963 at the very popular Mansion House St Patrick's Night Céilí. Caitríona comes from very impressive republican stock despite the fact that her grandfather was a Presbyterian and a British soldier from Ballywalter, County Down. Her father, Seán, had been sentenced to a year imprisonment in Mountjoy for storing IRA arms in his house in May 1928. Her mother's (Kathleen) grandfather, Joseph Hickey from the Strawberry Beds in County Dublin, was a Fenian and had fought in the Battle of Tallaght in 1867. Kathleen's uncle was Michael Mallin of the Irish Citizen Army who was executed in May 1916 for being the Officer Commanding in St Stephens Green and the Royal College of Surgeons. Fr Joseph Mallin, aged 96, is a Jesuit priest in Hong Kong and is the youngest son of Michael. He represents the last direct link with that seminal historical event in Irish history being the only child still living of the executed 1916 leaders. Fr Joseph is a regular correspondent with me and we meet on his regular visits to Ireland to visit his nieces, nephews and their children.

National Land League

The contacts made between trade unionists and small farmers and cottiers held out the prospect for something even bigger. Peadar's dream was the creation of a nexus between workers in urban areas and small farmers and landless people in the countryside. He believed that their coming together could challenge the rich industrialists as the dominant tier in Irish society. The opportunity to develop these theories came via a letter from Ned Gilligan, Secretary of Cullion Land Club. (Cullion is a townland a few miles outside Mullingar, County Westmeath.) Ned sought support from Fr McDyer who forwarded the letter to Peadar.

The Cullion Land Club was set up by Ned Gilligan and some friends and it was not long before it developed into the National Land League covering the counties of Westmeath, Kildare, Meath, Roscommon, Galway, Mayo, Cork, Tipperary and part of Offaly. The law of the land at the time was governed by the Land Acts which sought to redress congestion where many smallholders lived on small parcels of land while neighbouring large tracts of land lay idle in the hands of a rich minority. In the case of Cullion it was the Duke of Mecklenburg, a German cement magnate and owner of some 1,800 acres of land in Westmeath, who was the principal target. Another German, Herr Palm, owned 700 acres and the Irish-born Dr O'Malley had 600 acres. O'Malley took the Land Commission to court to prevent their proposed taking of some of his land but failed in his action. The commission had extraordinary legal power over the transfer of ownership of farmland which rivalled that enjoyed by socialist countries in eastern Europe. It could serve notice on owners of large acreages that they intended to acquire the land compulsorily for distribution among neighbouring smallholders and that they would pay a price independently of the market. The Cullion Land Club at the outset had completed a survey establishing that 300 young farmers could be set up on farms of land if the Commission took over the sprawling estates acquired by chequebook tycoons. The National Land League's campaign created over 200 new farms. It was a great achievement.

The new National Land League would differ from previous small farmer organisations in that the small farmers would actively pursue support from urban dwellers and trade unionists in particular. Peadar O'Donnell's booklet *The Role of the Industrial Worker* became a kind of bible for us. It outlined the leading role that needed to be played by workers in any campaign to impress their needs and vision on society. They could not do so without the support of country people with whom they had more in common than they thought. Contacts were made in Dublin at the highest level within the trade union movement, building on the relationships cemented during the cooperatives campaign. Senior union figures threw their considerable weight behind the demands of the small farmers.

The National Land League's activities took on more of a trade union approach to confront the large landowning tycoons. We picketed farm auctions in large numbers, organised demonstrations and canvassed politicians. Our strategy was to force the Land Commission to take over more of the large tracts of unused land. The other purpose of demonstrating at auctions was to deter would-be buyers from bidding in an effort to leave the way clear for the Land Commission. There were several celebrated cases of land acquisition by the Commission in County Westmeath. The leadership of the National Land League during those years was comprised of dedicated volunteers who gave freely of their time and talents. Peadar O'Donnell was honoured with lifelong presidency and I was their 'man in Dublin' with the title of Public Relations Officer (PRO). We published our own monthly newspaper, *The Countryman*, which I edited and which enjoyed widespread circulation among small farmers at the time. We even managed to have two councillors elected, Dan McCarthy in Westmeath and Peter Murphy in Longford.

Ireland's entry into the Common Market was such a financial bonanza for farmers that it became difficult to maintain the momentum we had built up. The other farming organisations were in favour of the Common Market while the trade union movement and small farmer groups were against joining. The influx of money into agriculture was the price paid for their votes and the farmers enjoyed unprecedented wealth in the early years. Not long after, the

National Land League was wound up. It was an idea for its
time and it is a great pity that events did not permit its natural
development. It would have profited the people of Ireland
greatly. Many small farmers and cottiers benefited from the
distribution of land and that would not have happened
without us. There was success in radicalising many areas of
rural Ireland and indeed the Labour Party benefited most from
this new 'constituency'. For example, a past president of the
National Land League, Dan McCarthy, is a Labour Party
councillor in Westmeath.

A Unique Man and Friend

Peadar O'Donnell led an astonishing life. He was a teacher, a
trade union organiser, an IRA soldier in the War of
Independence, a prisoner, an escapee, a soldier of the Republic
during the Civil War when he took the anti-Treaty side, a
member of the IRA Executive, an author, a playwright, an
editor and founder of the famous literary magazine *The Bell*
and above all a skilled agitator. He was an honest man of great
integrity. He thought as a socialist and acted accordingly and
always stood up for the underdog and underprivileged.

When he died at the age of ninety-three a light went out
for ever in our lives. I mourned him like I did my own father.
Peadar had nominated me as his executor for his will with his
nephew Doctor James O'Donnell and we arranged his affairs
as instructed. He explained that he wanted to be cremated, his
ashes buried in Swinford, County Mayo, and a notice put in
the paper in the days after to say that it had occurred. He did
not want any church ceremony nor priestly eulogy as his
comrades all those years ago had been denied that right.

Peadar's popularity meant that it would be impossible to
keep the news of his death a secret. In the early days of May
1986 word had spread that he was very ill and I knew that his
last wishes could not be accommodated in full. On 13 May I
was called to the hospital to be told of his passing and not long
after I arrived home I heard the details of his death on the

radio. With his son Peadar Joe we arranged for his body to be taken to a funeral home in Thomas Street, Dublin.

The following day we went to Glasnevin where a crowd had gathered beside the church where the remains of those about to be cremated are brought. The man in charge of the mortuary asked me if there would be prayers, to which I replied 'No.' Would there be a speech, music or poetry? 'No.' He looked surprised and said something to the effect that this was most unusual. He explained the procedure, that at the designated time he would press a button and the conveyor belt would carry the coffin behind the curtains and thereafter transport it to the crematorium. I asked him to wait for a signal from me before proceeding. I waited for as many people as possible to arrive before signalling. Many of those in attendance were disappointed, but I was determined to carry out Peadar's wishes faithfully.

The journey of his ashes to Swinford was like the homecoming of a prince. He was welcomed in Mullingar and other parts of Westmeath and Longford by crowds of small farmers from the National Land League. The word had gone out that we were travelling westward and we stopped here and there at villages where people had gathered to pay their respects. In Swinford his ashes were placed by his son Peadar Joe in the O'Donel family grave beside his beloved Lile. When Lile was buried there in 1969 Peadar had her name and his inscribed on the headstone.

While visiting Salvation Army hostels in England some years previously Peadar had met an old man from Mayo who told him that Peadar O'Donnell was dead and buried in Swinford. Peadar revealed his identity, explaining that he had authorised his name to go on the headstone years before. The man thought about this for a minute. 'The world is upside down,' he said. 'So now you can't even believe what you read on a headstone!'

EPILOGUE

I had reported back to the IRA in January 1961, a year before
the campaign had been called off, and had been welcomed
and sheltered by them for a number of weeks. But despite my
seeking medium-term refuge in a well-known and dedicated
republican house in Cork, my connections with the republican
movement weakened. There were a number of reasons for this.
First, the injuries I received in my escape left me in a very
debilitated state so it was difficult, if not impossible, to be
passionate about anything other than trying to get better. I had
been attending various hospitals in Cork and had established
a connection with the local republican movement only for
specific events and with named friends. But I had not much
energy to offer. Second, the movement was attempting to
resurrect itself after the failed Operation Harvest and the
general and local election results reflected its very poor
standing among the public. There was no grand recruiting
campaign at the time; indeed the movement lost many
members during those years. It was struggling to understand
its own role in Irish affairs.

As my fitness improved I gave over my spare time to
Pádraig Ó Síocháin's CARA organisation and even more to
Críostóir de Baróid's Scéim na gCeardcumann. There was
great excitement and energy in those groups since we
promoted Gaelic culture in language, song and dance with the
very attractive added dimension of special lectures on
historical and topical subjects that were very well attended. I

was also a founder member in Dublin. There was immense satisfaction as we drew our numbers from the Dublin trade union movement which meant that it was the opposite of elitist – a charge often levelled at Irish-speaking groups.

These activities created a real connection with the people in the west of Ireland who were struggling for more investment and greater recognition of both their difficulties and potential. This in turn became the focus for my interests and those of close friends and workmates. The early to mid-1960s was an exciting time in the Republic of Ireland with the plan for economic expansion and the increase in wages for those in work. Despite the undoubted progress, the rallying calls were for better housing and work for those in need and for the people in the west of Ireland who had been neglected for generations. There were plenty of causes for young people like me to espouse, and we did.

With John F. Kennedy elected US President, the reforming Kruschev in power in Moscow and Pope John XXIII in the Vatican it was naively felt by many that world peace was imminent. And in the mid-1960s when there were unprecedented public acts of reconciliation between Captain Terence O'Neill, Prime Minister in Stormont, and Taoiseach Seán Lemass there was a real belief, which I shared, that there would never be an armed insurrection against the northern government again. However, the slow response and indeed opposition to the nationalists' specific demands for civil rights and the loyalist backlash against them, a response supported by most of the grandees of unionism, gave us an even more dysfunctional Six County state which descended almost into anarchy.

People everywhere were being drawn into it. The litany of carnage, hurt, division and injustices of that period on every side confirms my long-standing view that the British government was fundamentally to blame for this state of affairs. They should have acted much earlier, in the 1950s, to create a just society. I avoided being personally involved in the physical conflict just by chance and to a certain extent through having other commitments. Thus I never rejoined the IRA as many of my Crumlin Road comrades did at that crucial time, nor was I part of the bitter Provisional/Official split. I knew many on both sides and still meet with some of them from time to time. However, I was quite frankly appalled at the ruthlessness with which those feuds were carried out and the bitterness that informed them. I consider myself fortunate to have been outside it all.

'Once a republican, always a republican' is a truism that is often quoted and variations on the same theme are applied to other political and social groups worldwide. When the unjust imprisonment of Giuseppe Conlon and the Guildford Four, the Birmingham Six and the Winchester Three became the subject of public campaigns with large gatherings in Dublin, I was there. English public figures such as the lawyer Gareth Pierce, Mike Mansfield, Queen's Counsel, Tony Benn, MP, Chris Mullen, MP and a host of others were in attendance. Their sense of justice transcended any feeling of self protection or hopes of personal elevation. They were and are extraordinary English people. These campaigns eventually won out.

The treatment of his body and the funeral of the hunger striker Frank Stagg, whose death in Wakefield Prison was so reminiscent of that of Terence MacSwiney, the Cork Lord Mayor who died fifty-six years earlier in Brixton Prison, brought me into public conflict with Cosgrave's coalition government through the letters page of the *Irish Press*. This was the time of the 'heavy gang', and the draconian Emergency Powers legislation was in preparation. Not long after that Dr Conor Cruise O'Brien, Minister for Posts and Telegraphs, stated in an interview with the *Washington Post* that he intended to pursue the prosecution of the editor of the *Irish Press*, Tim Pat Coogan, for publishing letters critical of his government, showing his interviewer a drawerful of letters cut from the paper. As John Mulcahy said at the time, 'Here was

O'Brien with a drawer full of letters when we thought we were paying him to deliver them!'

The people overwhelmingly voted them out of office in 1977 and the Emergency Powers proposal was dropped. The 1981 hunger strikes resulting in ten dead prisoners 'lit another fire within the land'. Dying and dormant passions about the North among old and young republicans of no affiliation were brought to life by the unprecedented courage of these men and the total lack of compassion of the British government led by Margaret Thatcher. From my own prison experience and from many discussions with Peadar O'Donnell I was not in favour of such hunger strikes. Peadar contended that the longer the strikes continued the greater the scope for division among the hunger strikers and their families and friends. This was based on his own experience in Mountjoy. If prisoners, for whatever reasons, came off the strike they were liable for criticism from some families and friends of those still on hunger strike and no credit was given for their sacrifice to date. The result was usually a divided movement and good Volunteers lost forever from the struggle. However, like so many others I could not remain neutral in such a situation and supported the hunger strikers' demands during those awful months. Who would have thought that those sad deaths would become the catalyst for change and would result in an electoral strategy that has brought about peace and justice?

For thirty years I was not able to return to Omagh. One would have thought that an event that happened so many years previously would be consigned to history, but not for the British. In the meantime my father took ill and lingered for a long time before eventually dying in 1972. Some family friends intervened on my behalf and requested permission for me to travel home but it was rejected outright. I waited in Monaghan town with good friends while my wife and eldest son, Eoin, went across the border to the funeral. In the mid-1980s my mother was surprised to learn from a local tradesman that my 'Wanted' photograph was still on view as

British soldiers exited their barracks in Omagh.

My employers knew my situation and that travel to England, Scotland, Wales and Northern Ireland was not feasible for me. Over an extended period my role required me to attend meetings everywhere in Europe, including the UK, but I could not attend the latter. After many years the Chairman of the company I was working for asked me to establish if it were possible for me to travel to the UK on the company's behalf. An acquaintance of mine, a Belfast businessman, made an enquiry on my behalf and advised that I should not go through any politician and should only employ the services of a solicitor who was not associated with republicanism. So I approached the President of the Irish Law Society, who made an application for me to travel. It was initially rejected but eventually granted in 1986.

On 15 August 1998 an event took place that would stamp the name of Omagh indelibly on people's minds throughout the world. Twenty-nine innocent people and two unborn babies were indiscriminately blown to pieces by a bomb left in Market Street in the centre of the town. The culprits were the Real IRA. By using the title IRA in their claim of responsibility they were seeking the sanction of history for their barbarous act. Never was a claim so unjustified nor a cause so besmirched. The awful act was all the more diabolical as it was perpetrated during peace time and was designed to derail the rising hopes of the majority of Irish people who had voted overwhelmingly in favour of peace in the May 1998 referendum, North and South. It brought opprobrium on republicans of all shades and has left a lingering sense of shame. The last victim to die, well known to me, was Seán McGrath, whose family had a grocer's shop many years ago on the very street the bomb exploded. Seán was an altar boy and as he grew older he assisted in organising the many activities that we altar boys enjoyed. I would often meet him and his wife and family in Bundoran on summer holidays. Laurence Rushe, although younger than me, was at school at the same time and grieves openly for his wife, Elizabeth, as do all of the other families. They will never be forgotten.

Life continued and I found myself working professionally as a purchasing manager and planner and devoting some time to voluntary work in my neighbourhood and elsewhere.

It is over fifty years since I was imprisoned as a teenager and almost fifty since I escaped. My experience of prison equipped me to face any challenge in life with the knowledge that there were worse things that could happen. In a strange way it reduced any natural fear of the unknown that I might have had. The things I observed, the people I met in that bleak place shaped my approach to those who are deprived socially, financially and emotionally. These days, among other activities, I meet with a group of ex-combatants from both loyalist and republican backgrounds in a structured way to work together in a genuine effort to reduce sectarianism and create an 'us and us' rather than an 'us and them' society. My lifelong quest has been to promote community. A good community environment is a tremendous bulwark against isolation and loneliness. I am fortunate that for the past forty-two years I have lived with my wife and family in a pleasant, caring and supportive community on the edge of Dublin between the mountains and the harbour. My wish is that all the people of Ireland could aspire to live in such a community, one that will help them to meet the challenges of modern life. This wish is especially for those in the North in the coming years as they attempt to live in peace and harmony.

APPENDICES

APPENDIX I

Internees Between 1956 and 1961

The following list was compiled by Art Mac Eachaidh (Art McCaughey), former sacristan of the Catholic church in Dungannon and former internee in Crumlin Road Gaol. The list is of those interned in D Wing between December 1956 and March 1961. The names are replicated here (apart from the first three) exactly as Art wrote them and may not constitute a complete record of those interned. The names recorded are specifically those of men served with internment orders as distinct from detention orders, which were temporary. David Lewsley from Lurgan very kindly supplied a photocopy of this list. David was in A Wing at the same time as the author.

Paddy Smith, Republican Prisoner, Newry
P. J. Cunningham, Republican Prisoner, Newry
Eddie Burns, Republican Prisoner, Newry
Paddy Larkin, Bar Attendant, Belfast
Jerry McGuire, Dealer, Belfast
John McAlaskey, Farmer, Derrylaughan, Co. Tyrone
Seán Corr, Farmer/Fisherman, Ballylittle, Stewartstown, Co. Tyrone
Frank Cullen, Labourer, Coalisland
Patsy Quinn, Farmer, Ardboe, Co. Tyrone
James McGorry, Carpenter, Stewartstown, Co. Tyrone
Hugh Brady, Textile Worker, Lurgan
Barney Murphy, Farmer, Newbridge, Co. Tyrone
Cathal Grimes, Farmer, Pomeroy, Co. Tyrone
Dermot Casey, Electrician, Edendork
Seán McCormick, Shoe Repairer, Belfast
Frank Duggan, Labourer, Armagh
Art Thornberry, Student, Lurgan
Seán Cullen, Bricklayer, Coalisland, Co. Tyrone
Brendan Lennon, Bricklayer, Lurgan
Bob McMillan, Window Cleaner, Belfast

Patsy Duffy, Shop Attendant, Lurgan
Charles Devlin, Fisherman, Mountjoy, Co. Tyrone
Eddie McLaughlin, Steel Erector, Strabane
Dermot Smith, Apprentice Gardener, Strabane
Séamus McMahon, Storeman, Corgy, Ballymena
Gordon Walsh, Commercial Traveller, Belturbet, Co. Cavan
Leonard McGill, Barman, Lurgan
Jerry McGill, Farm Labourer, Lurgan
Jim McVeigh, Builder's Labourer, Derrymacash, Lurgan
Tom Fitzpatrick, Carpenter, Inniskeen, Co. Monaghan
Patsy McAlinden, Lorry Driver, Lurgan
Frank Rafferty, Farm Labourer, Mountnorris, Co. Armagh
Kevin O'Rourke, Bricklayer, Banbridge, Co. Down
Larry Mulholland, Builder's Labourer, Upperlands, Co. Derry
John Davey, Bulldozer Driver, Glaryford, Co. Antrim
Séamus Hoey, Shop Assistant, Inniskeen, Co. Monaghan
Pat Daly, Building Contractor, Inniskeen, Co. Monaghan
Peter McRory, Shop Assistant, Ballygawley, Co. Tyrone
Joe Campbell, Shoe Repairer, Newry
Liam Kelly, Machinist Engineer, Belfast
John McNeill, Sheep Farmer, Cushendun, Co. Antrim
Teddy O'Neill, Filleter, Belfast
Johnny McCluskey, Sheep Farmer, Dungiven, Co. Derry
John Francis McCluskey, Farmer, Dungiven, Co. Derry
James Ward, General Dealer, Belfast
Danny Moore, Sawmill Worker, Newry
James Loughran, Fowl Plucker, Lurgan
Dermot O'Haire, Builder's Labourer, Lurgan
Frank McLaughlin, Clerk, Strabane
Seán Keenan, Bookmaker's Clerk, Derry City
Seán Loughran, Apprentice Electrician, Dungannon
Thomas J. Quinn, Fisherman, Moortown, Co. Tyrone
Mick Kelly, Fisherman, Moortown, Co. Tyrone
Brendan Lennon, Bricklayer, Lurgan
Larry McGurk, Apprentice Welder, Belfast
Séamus McReynolds, Farmer, Dungiven, Co. Derry
Kevin McGill, Lorry Driver, Dungiven, Co. Derry
John McCusker, Farmer, Brackareilly, Co. Derry
Seán Duffy, Draughtsman, Newry
Cannus O'Kane, Forestry Worker, Dungiven, Co. Derry
Peter McGuinness, Commercial Traveller, Camlough, Co. Armagh
Aidan McKenna, Textile Worker, Lurgan
Matt Loy, Bricklayer, Newry

Billy McKee, Textile Worker, Belfast
Joe McGurk, Clerk, Belfast
Barney Boswell, Checker at Docks, Belfast
Ciarán O'Kane, University Student, Belfast
Patrick Doyle, Insurance Agent, Belfast
Barney McLaughlin, Labourer, Belfast
Art Kerr, Bread Server, Derry City
Patrick L. Doherty, Stained Glass Artist, Derry City
Gerard Doherty, Bread Server, Derry City
Seán Moore, Clerk, Newry
Billy O'Neill, Lorry Driver, Belfast
Patsy McGuinness, Fowl Plucker, Lurgan
Éamonn McConville, Milk Roundsman, Derrymacash, Lurgan
Ronnie McAlinden, Textile Worker, Lurgan
Leo Martin, Tiler, Belfast
Eugene Moore, Butcher's Apprentice, Newry
Ivor Bell, Plasterer, Belfast
Jimmy Martin, Scaffolder, Belfast
Tommy McGuire, Bookmaker, Belfast
Gerry Higginbothem, Clerk, Dublin
Joseph Rooney, Clerk, Newry
Peter Quinn, Plumber, Belfast
Paddy McConnell, Hod Carrier, Belfast
Pat Shivers, Brickyard Worker, Toomebridge, Co. Antrim
Denis Toner, Cable Layer, Belfast
Manuel Davis, Cable Jointer, Belfast
Malachy O'Reilly, Labourer, Farmer, Co. Fermanagh
Paddy Corey, Labourer, Brackaville, Coalisland, Co. Tyrone
Brendan McHenry, Farmer, Dungiven, Co. Derry
Joe Cahill, Carpenter, Belfast
Liam McMillan, Scaffolding Erector, Belfast
Frank Cahill, Plastic Moulder, Belfast
Hugh O'Neill, Architect Student, Belfast
Pearse Martin, Post Office Worker, Belfast
James Gallagher, Bricklayer, Omagh
Paddy (Joe) McClean, Teacher, Beragh, Co. Tyrone
Brendan McNamee, Poultry Dealer, Sixmilecross, Co. Tyrone
Tommy Toner, Farmer, Dungiven, Co. Derry
Seán Fitzpatrick, Newry
Bobby McKnight, Storeman, Belfast
Peter O'Neill, Farm Labourer, Moortown, Co. Tyrone
Jimmy Heslop, Labourer, Belfast
Seán Duffy, Sawmill Worker, Newry

Joseph Quinn, Farm Labourer, Ardboe, Co. Tyrone
Malachy McBurney, Tailor, Belfast
Seán McKearney, Electrician, Belfast
Seán Ó Cearnaigh, Language Worker, Belfast
Brendan O'Reilly, Upholsterer, Belfast
Art Mac Eachaidh, Sacristan, Dungannon
James Savage, Creamery Worker, Newry
Dominic Loy, Apprentice Butcher, Newry
Charles Young, Farmer, Ballinderry, Co. Derry
Brendan Foley, Shop Assistant, Dungannon
Christopher Loy, Council Worker, Water Dept, Newry
Jerry Mulligan, Compositor, Newry
Vincent McCormack, Apprentice Plumber, Newry
Adam McIlhatton, Car Driver, Belfast
Desmond Gourly, Farmer, Cookstown, Co. Tyrone
Teddy Devlin, Textile Worker, Dungannon
Joe McPharland, Abattoir Worker, Belfast
Paddy J. Mullan, Insurance Agent, Cookstown, Co. Tyrone
Colm McCusker, Builder's Labourer, Maghera, Co. Derry
Frank Moore, Builder's Labourer, Newry
Charles McGlinchy, Farmer, Strabane
Paddy Devlin, Railway Worker, Dungannon
James O'Connor, Farmer, Desertmartin, Co. Derry
Brian Cassidy, Lorry Driver, Desertmartin, Co. Derry
Denis Cassidy, Farmer, Maghera, Co. Derry
James Morgan, Sailor, Newry
Frank McRogan, Bricklayer, Belfast
Séamus Devlin, Farmer, The Loop, Co. Derry
Seán McNally, Plasterer, Belfast
Patsy Molloy, Farmer, Brackareilly, Co. Derry
Barney Young, Farmer, Ballinderry, Co. Derry
Jack Cassidy, Farmer, Maghera, Co. Derry
James O'Sullivan, Labourer, Belfast
Patrick McManus, Textile Worker, Newry
James Steele, Plasterer, Bread Server, Belfast
James Drumm, Moulder, Belfast
Liam Mulholland, Gas Worker, Belfast
Dominic Adams, Barber, Belfast
Seán McSorley, Builder's Labourer, Ballygawley, Co. Tyrone
John McEldowney, Shop Assistant, Maghera, Co. Derry
Danny O'Donnell, Engine Driver, Derry
Danny Devlin, Carpenter, Annaghaboe, Coalisland
William Holden, Roof Worker, Belfast

Seán Killeen, Plastic Moulder, Belfast
Jimmy O'Hare, Bookmaker's Clerk, Belfast
Seán Gibson, Mineral Water Worker, Belfast
John O'Hagan, Building Contractor, Desertmartin, Co. Derry
Malachy Murray, Bricklayer, Belfast
Art McMillan, Glassmaker, Belfast
Tom Heenan, Fitter, Belfast
Jack Hegarty, Poultry Farmer, Ballinasrceen, Co. Derry
Frank MacAirt, Crane Operator, Belfast
Séamus Ramsay, Bus Body Builder, Derry City
Danny McAlinden, Van Driver, Belfast
Tom O'Connor, Apprentice Photographer, Dungannon
Brendan Lavery, Solicitor's Clerk, Lurgan
John O'Hagan, Grocer, Mechanic, Mullagabawn, Co. Armagh
Pat Murtagh, Electrician, Jerrets Pass, Co. Armagh
Sammy O'Hanlon, Electrician, Belfast
Tom McGill, Fitter, Belfast
Séamus Kavanagh, Clerk of Works, Lurgan
Liam Kennedy, Bookmaker's Clerk, Belfast
Leo McCormick, Labourer, Dublin
Frank Maguire, Publican, Lisnaskea, Co. Fermanagh
David Ramsay, Press Operator, Derry City
Joe Haughian, Fowl Plucker, Lurgan
Seán O'Gallagher, Railway Worker, Derry City
Seán Dullaghan, French Polisher, Belfast
Gerry McCotter, Ship Steward, Belfast
Frank Donnelly, Labourer, Brackareilly, Co. Derry
Phil Campbell, Labourer, Belfast
Bob McCurry, Hotel Worker, Belfast
Brendan Mallon, Farmer, Moortown, Co. Tyrone
Mick McAleese, Textile Worker, Lurgan
James McWilliams, Teacher, Omagh
Joe McCallion, Builder's Labourer, Strabane
Mick Kane, Carpenter, Strabane
Tommy Mellon, Plumber, Derry City
Jimmy Jameson, Labourer, Belfast
Jerry Robinson, Shop Floor Worker, Belfast
Seán McParland, Linen Printer, Belfast
Liam McParland, Cabinet Maker, Belfast
Kevin Mallon, Labourer, Coalisland, Co. Tyrone
Francis Talbot, Textile Worker, Coalisland, Co. Tyrone
Ben McHugh, Creamery Worker, Swanlinbar, Co. Cavan
Seán Woods, Labourer, Omagh

Seán Collins, Builder's Labourer, Lavey, Co. Derry
James McKenna, Lorry Driver, Brackareilly, Co. Derry
Derek Hystead, Labourer, Maghera, Co. Derry
Laurence Kane, Carpenter, Strabane
James McElduff, Farmer, Mountfield, Omagh
Hugh Dunne, Projectionist, Strabane
Danny Morgan, Bookmaker's Clerk, Belfast
Tony Murray, Fitter in Shipyard, Belfast
Hugh Kelly, Farm Labourer, Ardboe, Co. Tyrone
Jim McGuckin, Farm Labourer, Ardboe, Co. Tyrone
Mick Mullan, Blacksmith, Strabane
Paddy Coyle, Carpenter, Greencastle, Co. Tyrone
Peter Monaghan, Dunamore, Cookstown, Co. Tyrone
Eddie Dean, Leather Worker, Belfast

Bridie O'Neill from Belfast was the only woman served with an internment order during these years and was incarcerated in Armagh Gaol on her own.

APPENDIX II

List of Long-Term* Sentenced IRA Prisoners, 1953-60

The original list was complied by Éamon Timoney from Derry city who was a good friend of the author. Christian names and length of sentences have been added and also several names which had been omitted from the original. After his release Éamon emigrated to New York and later returned to Liverpool where he died in 1987. I am grateful to An Eochair's (Ex-Prisoner Support Group) Seán Curry who provided a photocopy of this list.

Year Imprisoned	Sentence (years)	Name	Home Town	Age	Occupation
1953	5	Joe Campbell	Newry	30	Shoemaker
1954	4	Leo McCormack	Dublin	36	Labourer
	12	Éamonn Boyce	Dublin	28	Bus Conductor
	10	Tom Mitchell	Dublin	23	Brick Layer
	10	Paddy Kearney	Dublin	28	Bus Conductor
	10	Jack McCabe	Dublin	34	Labourer
	10	Phil Clarke	Dublin	21	Student
	10	Liam Mulcahy	Cork	28	Baker
	10	Seán O'Callaghan	Cork	21	Audit Clerk
	10	Seán Hegarty	Cork	21	P.O. Linesman

* Serving sentences in excess of three years.

Year Imprisoned	Sentence (years)	Name	Home Town	Age	Occupation
1954	4	Hugh Brady	Lurgan	28	Poultry Worker
	5	Kevin O'Rourke	Banbridge	30	Brick Layer
1956	12	Anthony Cooney	Cork	21	P.O. Clerk
	10	Jimmy Linehan	Cork	20	Labourer
	10	Willie Gough	Cork	20	Driver
	10	Séamus Houston	Keady	23	Electrician
	8	Jim Smith	Bessbrook	18	Draughtsman
	8	John Kelly	Belfast	20	Marine Engineer
1956	8	David Lewsley	Lurgan	20	Baker
	8	John Madden	Cork	20	Brick Layer
	3	Peter Monaghan	Dunamore	21	Farmer
1957	8	Paddy Constantine	Dublin	28	Carpenter
	8	Peter Duffy	Dundalk	41	Factory Machinist
	8	Séamus Hand	Dundalk	23	Electrician
	8	Pat Shaw	Dundalk	20	Factory Machinist
	8	Gabriel Loy	Newry	20	Factory Machinist
	8	Anthony Loy	Newry	25	Plumber
	8	Tommy Kearns	Newry	20	Van Salesman
	6	Piaras Ó Dubháil	Dublin	27	Chemist's Assistant
	5	Paddy Hodgins	Dublin	21	Woodworker
	4	Phil McStravick	Lurgan	24	Labourer
	4	Des O'Hagan	Belfast	23	Journalist
	4	Paddy McGrogan	Belfast	24	Heating Engineer
	4	Tommy Fearon	Belfast	20	Grocer's Assistant
	6	Jimmy Corbett	Belfast	21	Labourer
	10	Éamon Timoney	Derry	29	Railway Clerk
	10	Packy Dan O'Kane	Dungiven	32	Farmer
	10	Paddy Fox	Derry	23	Driver
	6	Matt Monaghan	Derry	20	Mechanic
	6	Larry McGowan	Derry	19	Factory Machinist
	3	Peter Gillespie	Draperstown	26	Farmer

Year Imprisoned	Sentence (years)	Name	Home Town	Age	Occupation
1957	4	Cyril Mellon	Sion Mills	23	Publican
	10	Danny Donnelly	Omagh	18	Student
	8	Seán McHugh	Beragh	27	Carpenter
	6	Jim Devlin	Omagh	25	Farmer
	5	Paddy Devlin	Omagh	20	Labourer
	4	Fergus McCabe	Omagh	17	Barman
	4	Arthur McCarroll	Omagh	18	Brick Layer
	4	Frank Cullen	Omagh	18	Labourer
	4	Hugh Darcy	Omagh	18	Farmer
	5	Jim Darcy	Omagh	19	Farmer
	12	Tommy McCool	Derry	29	Labourer
	10	Larry McKinney	Derry	20	Shirt-Cutter
	14	Kevin Mallon	Coalisland	24	Labourer
	8	Frank Talbot	Coalisland	22	Factory Machinist
	15	Eddie Mulholland	Lurgan	18	Poultry Packer
	8	John Robinson	Coalisland	24	Fisherman
	10	Jim O'Donnell	Coalisland	24	Labourer
	10	Barney O'Neill	Coalisland	31	Driver
	5	John Pat Herron	Coalisland	34	Farmer
	5	Paddy O'Neill	Coalisland	24	Farmer
	5	Seán O'Neill	Coalisland	23	Farmer
	6	Tommy O'Malley	Belfast	51	Labourer
	5	Paddy Collins	Belfast	40	Labourer
1958	5	Séamus McRory	Ballymena	26	Printer
	5	Hugh McRory	Ballymena	22	Printer
	5	Jimmy McKernan	Ballymena	22	Plumber
	5	Brian Loughran	Ballymena	29	Van Salesman
	5	Séamus Loughran	Ballymena	23	Gardener
	6	Tommy O'Kane	Belfast	27	Labourer
	5	Kevin Carson	Enniskillen	22	Civil Servant
	5	Éamonn Goodwin	Enniskillen	17	Joiner
	5	Frank Goodwin	Enniskillen	19	Electrician
	5	Harry Martin	Enniskillen	24	Carpenter
	5	Joe Owens	Enniskillen	22	Carpenter
	14	Paddy Traynor	Monaghan	25	Farmer
	14	Denis Foley	Tralee	18	Clerk
	14	Tony Meade	Limerick	20	Clerk
	14	Willie Reilly	Armagh	19	Labourer
	3	Joe Quinn	Newry	19	Labourer

Year Imprisoned	Sentence (years)	Name	Home Town	Age	Occupation
1958	8	Noel McLaughlin	Newry	19	Lorry Driver
1959	3	Frank Lanney	Castleblaney	33	Clerk
	5	Mick Daly	Crossmaglen	26	Farmer
	5	Owen Carraher	Crossmaglen	25	Farmer
	5	Frank McArdle	Newry	21	Seaman
	3	Patrick Loy	Newry	18	Factory Machinist
	5	John Healy	Newry	18	Grocer's Assistant
1959	4	Seán Garland	Dublin	24	Labourer
	9	Gerry Haughian	Lurgan	21	Poultry Packer
	10	Liam Flanagan	Maghera	22	Labourer
	8	J. B. (Joe) O'Hagan	Lurgan	36	Businessman
1960	10	Daithí Ó Conaill	Cork	22	Carpenter
	14	Don McPhillips	Lurgan	24	Labourer
	14	David Egan	Galway	24	Grocer's Assistant
	12	Tony Cosgrove	Belfast	18	Carpenter
	12	Bobby Murray	Belfast	18	Sheet Metal Worker

APPENDIX III

IRA Roll of Honour, 1956–62

Name	Died	Home Town
Feargal O'Hanlon	1 January 1957	Monaghan
Seán Sabhat (Seán South)	1 January 1957	Limerick
Paul Smith	11 November 1957	Armagh
Oliver Craven	11 November 1957	Down
Patrick Parle	11 November 1957	Wexford
George Keegan	11 November 1957	Wexford
Michael Waters	11 November 1957	Louth
Pat McManus	15 July 1958	Cavan
Séamus Crossan	24 August 1958	Fermanagh
John Duffy	7 May 1960	Derry

APPENDIX IV

RUC Roll of Honour, 1956–62

Name	Died	Place Killed
Constable John Scally	30 December 1956	Fermanagh
Constable T. C. J. Gregg	4 July 1957	Armagh
Constable H. B. Ross	17 July 1958	Armagh
Sergeant A. J. Ovens	17 August 1957	Tyrone
Constable N. J. C. Anderson	27 January 1961	Fermanagh
Constable W. J. Hunter	12 November 1961	Armagh

Source: www.ukpolice.org/rucroll/index.htm

INDEX

Eden, Sir Anthony 56
Edentubber 87
Edergole 28
Elliot, Constable William 70
Elwyn-Jones 88
Enniskillen 54
EOKA 52, 100
Erin Foods 176
Eskra 27, 28, 63, 70
European Works Council 169, 170
Evening Press 163

Fannin, District Inspector 14
Farrell, Michael 92
Faulkner, Brian 22
Feeley, John 177
Fenians 92
Fermanagh 28, 31, 32, 51, 54–56, 63, 82, 92
Ferris, Charlie 53
Fianna Fáil 56, 98, 157
Fine Gael 157
Fintona 27, 63
Fitzgerald, Séamus 157
Flags & Emblems Bill 42, 45, 55
Flanagan, Denis 41
Flanagan, Sergeant 47, 48
Flanagan, Liam 102
Flanagan, Peter 48
FLN 52, 101
Fogarty, Bishop Joseph 175
Foster, John 20
Fox, John Collins 29
Free State 32
Freud, Sir Clement 173, 174

GAA 32, 123
Gallagher, Adrian 178
Gallagher, James 28
Gallagher, Michael ('Red Mick') 28–31
Gardaí 56, 57, 104, 130, 149, 150, 157
Garland, Seán 77, 101–103
GCE 80, 81
Gifford family 30
Gilligan, Ned 180
Gilroy, Freddy 85
Gleeson, Áine 154

Gleeson, Dan 154
Gleeson, Maureen 154
Gleeson, Willie 53
Glenhordial 53
Glenravel Street Station 11
Goodwin, Éamonn 82
Goodwin, Frank 82
Gough, Owen 152
Goulding, Cathal 153, 154
Grace Brothers 164, 166, 167
Greece 52, 100, 171
Greencastle 53
Guildford Four 186

Hamill, Brother J. D. 38
Hamill, Mickey, 38
Harlay, Charlie 53
Haughey, Charles 76, 153, 178
Haughian, Gerry 96
Haughian, Pat 64
Hayman-Joyce, Sir Robert 173
HB Ice Cream 164, 167, 168
Headon, Tommy 164
Hegarty, Mrs 157
Henderson, John 53
Hickey, Joseph 179
Hickson, John 171
Higginbothem, Gerry 53, 61
Hillery, Patrick 173
Hola Camp 99
Holmes, Nathaniel 70
Hopkins, County Inspector 13
Hughes Dairies 167
Humphreys, Dick 155
Humphreys, Emmett 155
Humphreys, Evelyn 155
Humphreys, Síghle 155

IDA 172
INLA 96
IRA 27–30, 32, 44–46, 47, 48, 51, 52, 55, 56, 60, 62–64, 66, 76–79, 86, 89, 95, 96, 99, 103, 104, 127, 129, 142, 144, 151–154, 161, 179, 182, 184, 188
    Continuity 96
    Official 77, 96, 154